JAMES STOCK

James Stock lives in Manchester with Nancy Green, a Homoeopath, and their two children. For *Blue Night in the Heart of the West* he won the 1992 George Devine Award. He was Playwright in Residence at Contact Theatre, Manchester in 1990-1, on an Arts Council Bursary; and at the Royal Shakespeare Company in 1992-3, on a Thames Television Bursary. His plays include *A Prick-Song for the New Leviathan* (Plain Clothes Productions, Old Red Lion, 1990); *The Shaming of Bright Millar* (Contact Theatre, Manchester, 1991); *Blue Night in the Heart of the West* (Plain Clothes Productions, The Bush, and British tour, 1991; Plain Clothes Productions, Traverse Theatre, Edinburgh, 1993; Théâtre de l'Instant, Brest; Théâtre de la Cité Internationale, Paris; Théâtre Garonne, Toulouse, 1995); *Star-Gazy Pie and Sauerkraut* (Royal Court Theatre Upstairs, 1995). For BBC Radio he has written *Kissing the Gargoyle* (1994), for which he was joint winner of the 1995 Richard Imison Award; and *Ron Koop's Last Roadshow* (1995), a live drive-in radio road movie.

A selection of other volumes in this series

Jez Butterworth
MOJO

Caryl Churchill
CHURCHILL: SHORTS
CLOUD NINE
ICECREAM
LIGHT SHINING IN
    BUCKINGHAMSHIRE
MAD FOREST
THE SKRIKER
TRAPS
THYESTES
    (trans from Seneca)

Ariel Dorfman
DEATH AND THE MAIDEN
READER

David Edgar
EDGAR: SHORTS
PENTECOST
THE SHAPE OF THE TABLE
THE STRANGE CASE OF DR
    JEKYLL AND MR HYDE

Kevin Elyot
MY NIGHT WITH REG

Tony Kushner
ANGELS IN AMERICA
    Parts One and Two

Clare McIntyre
MY HEART'S A SUITCASE
    & LOW LEVEL PANIC

Arthur Miller
PLAYING FOR TIME

Rona Munro
IT'S YOUR TURN TO
    CLEAN THE STAIR
THE MAIDEN STONE

Phyllis Nagy
BUTTERFLY KISS
THE STRIP

Eugene O'Neill
AH! WILDERNESS
ANNA CHRISTIE &
    THE EMPEROR JONES
DESIRE UNDER THE ELMS
THE HAIRY APE &
    ALL GOD'S CHILLUN
THE ICEMAN COMETH
LONG DAY'S JOURNEY
    INTO NIGHT
A MOON FOR THE
    MISBEGOTTEN
MOURNING BECOMES
    ELECTRA
STRANGE INTERLUDE
A TOUCH OF THE POET

James Stock

STAR-GAZY PIE

Two Plays

Blue Night in the Heart
of the West

AND

Star-Gazy Pie and Sauerkraut

LONDON

NICK HERN BOOKS

A Nick Hern Book

Star-Gazy Pie first published in 1995 as an original paperback by
Nick Hern Books Ltd, 14 Larden Road, London W3 7ST

Blue Night in the Heart of the West copyright © 1995 James Stock
Star-Gazy Pie and Sauerkraut copyright © 1995 James Stock
Introductory material © 1995 James Stock

Lines from 'Distant Howling' by Miroslav Holub in
On the Contrary and Other Poems, published by Bloodaxe, 1984

Front cover: from *Cod on the Beach* by J.M.W. Turner,
watercolour and gouache on paper, *c.* 1835

Typeset by Country Setting, Woodchurch, Kent TN26 3TB
Printed and bound by Athenaeum Press, Ltd.,
Gateshead, Tyne & Wear.

A CIP catalogue record for this book is available from
the British Library

ISBN 1 85459 293 9

BLUE NIGHT IN THE HEART OF THE WEST

For Matthew and Virginia

'the disease of feeling germed'

Thomas Hardy

Note

I met Matthew Zajac at the Royal Exchange in Manchester around
1988. He was in a Ben Jonson play. I was in a group writing seven-
minute plays with Iain Heggie. We were in a rehearsal room
asking actors from the company to act out our little pieces for us.
No-one was going up to Matthew, and no-one was coming up to
me, so we both felt like the last ones to get picked for football in
the playground. He looked a bit like Clint Eastwood, except for his
hair, which was just like Harvey Keitel's in *Taxi Driver*. And he
sort of shuffled about like Chris Waddle. I thought this was an
irresistible combination, so I showed him my little piece about a
Cornish plumber and how the feeding bottle was invented, and
discovered he was from Inverness. 'Can you do a Cornish plumber
for me?' 'Aye, no problem, pal.' Another writer, Charlotte Keatley,
said we should cut the speech about the feeding bottle out, so we
did. I ended up using it in *Star-Gazy Pie and Sauerkraut*, but
unfortunately Charlotte saw this as well and told me it just wasn't
working. She must really hate that speech. I said, 'But it's fascinating.' I knew it was fascinating because Mark Wing-Davey, who
directed the play, had told me so that very morning, seconds before
he'd suggested we cut it out, too. Well I caved in. So I've still got
this unspeakable (but fascinating) speech I've been trying to get
into a play for years. I intend to put it in everything now as a
matter of course, so I can be the first to suggest to the directors that
it's cut. This will surely seduce them into thinking I'm not only
uncommonly willing to take stuff out, but also a shrewd judge of
the unspeakable.

A year after we met, Matthew set up a company called 'Plain
Clothes' with some friends. He asked me for a play. I said 'Can
you do a 17th-century Communist from Norfolk, big fan of
Cromwell?' 'Aye, no problem.' I gave him *A Prick-Song for the
New Leviathan*. I'd just seen the Bill Douglas film, *Comrades*, so
I said, 'Try to get the bloke who plays George Loveless to do
Thomas Hobbes.' 'What's his name?' 'Don't know.' They found
him somehow. Rob Soans. Luckily for us he was one of those
actors who don't even raise an eyebrow when you ask them to help
pay the rent at The Old Red Lion.

After that 'Plain Clothes' got some money from the Arts Council,
which helped to cover the cost of writing hundreds of letters to

people asking them for money. If they surrendered some they instantly became 'angels'. I got some of that money to write *Blue Night in the Heart of the West*. I'm rather proud and rather flattered to have been commissioned by angels. I tried to make a character specially for Matthew: a tall, gullible, friendly humanist from the Highlands. Inverness, in fact. I said, 'Right up your street, eh?' He said, 'I can't do this. This isn't me. We're not like that.'

The play wasn't coming in to Manchester (where I live), so the director, Sallie Aprahamian, dragged me down to London to finish it in her flat. Well, to start it, really. I mean I'd done all the thinking. It was only the writing. I had four weeks. I walked into Crouch End and bought some tapes. Most of *Blue Night* was written listening to 'Blood' by This Mortal Coil, which probably explains a lot.

The company wound up rehearsing for well over a week without knowing how the play was going to end. And it was pretty clear to them I was the wrong person to ask. I can't do proper scenarios, they seem to replace the crazed logic of a story with something too mechanical and well-oiled, some vehicle pre-programmed to go somewhere. In short, they spoil the fun. So I'd certainly fail the Henrik Ibsen test of a playwright. But I suppose it must be disconcerting for a company already in rehearsal to hear the writer babbling incoherently about what might happen if it sort of wants to go that way. In the circumstances, I was bowled over by everyone's kindness and patience and understanding. It was a happy company, nothing threw them. Of course I found out later how murderous and mutinous they were really feeling. Great actors, all of them. Had me fooled.

JAMES STOCK
Manchester, September 1995

Characters

RUTH SHREVEPORT (46)
CARL SHREVEPORT (30)
KRISTIN SHREVEPORT (30)
DANIEL SHREVEPORT (46)
ANDREW MacALPINE (26)
OLD MAN
WOMAN (New York)
POLISH WOMAN (New York)
MAN (New York)
WAITRESS (Reno)
PRIEST

It is possible to perform the play with four actors, doubling parts as follows:

1 – RUTH / POLISH WOMAN / WAITRESS
2 – CARL / OLD MAN / MAN / PRIEST
3 – KRISTIN / WOMAN
4 – ANDREW / DANIEL

Blue Night in the Heart of the West was first performed by Plain Clothes Productions at the Bush Theatre, London, on 28 August 1991. The cast was as follows:

CARL / OLD MAN / MAN / PRIEST	Tom Mannion
KRISTIN / WOMAN	Virginia Radcliffe
RUTH / POLISH WOMAN / WAITRESS	Lynne Verrall
ANDREW / DANIEL	Matthew Zajac

Director Sallie Aprahamian
Designer Anthony Lamble
Music Andrew Dodge

Author's Note

'Landscaping the Mind' is a book that has not yet been written and there is no town called Epiphany in the State of Iowa. I find this strange on both counts.

PART ONE

ONE

nitrates

Independence Day on the Shreveport farm in Iowa. 4 a.m.
Vast landscape, endless plain. RUTH and CARL in the middle
of a cornfield.

CARL holding RUTH high in embrace, head buried in her
stomach. RUTH's legs wrapped round him, skirts billowing.
A dance, evolving into passionate, abandoned fuck.

RUTH tears at CARL's jeans, pushing them down. They fall to the
ground. RUTH twists in the dirt, kneeling. CARL falls over
himself in his urgency, scrambling to climb in behind her. When it
is over, a long silence.

RUTH splayed out, face against the ground. CARL crawls, jeans
around his ankles, to waiting can of beer.

CARL. So anyway he says to me 'You know boy, this is one
  helluva country, the finest, the biggest and the best'. And all I
  said was, 'How d'you figure a thing like that, Sam? Can you
  measure it?' And all of a sudden he's grabbing hold of me right
  there in the store, and I'm thinking Jesus Christ this guy's
  gonna explode in my face, he's all red and wheezing like a sick
  cow – and he says, 'Do you want this country overrun, boy? Is
  that what you want for your children? Because that is what's
  gonna happen unless we do something about it'. And I said,
  'Do what, Sam?' And he says, he says, listen to this, he says,
  'There are people in the world boy, who don't know, they don't
  know the first fucking thing – how to behave, how to believe,
  how to live in their own fucking land – and these people, who'd
  be dead if there was any justice left, are gonna be wandering
  our land and they won't even understand it – the entire fucking
  landscape's gonna be incomprehensible to them.' He's choking
  me, the son of a bitch, so I said, 'All right, Sam, let go of my
  shirt'. But now he's yelling something about what you need to
  survive out here is a buffalo mentality and I'm thinking ain't
  that the truth 'cos the old bastard's laying buffalo breath all
  over me. He's practically eating my nose. 'The only way to be
  certain is to send our boys out there to start dealing with all that
  foreign people pollution 'fore it comes anywhere near us.'

CARL *chuckles, drinks, offers the can to* RUTH.

You want a beer – ?

RUTH *lies still. Beat.*

So there I am, and I'm saying, 'Okay, Sam, good point, good
point – but, well, I don't know, it seems a mite energetic, Sam,
a little too Nietzschean for my taste. You see, Sam, I'm more of
a wait and see kinda guy. Play every experience as it comes.
Don't go looking for trouble, you know what I mean?' So then
he relaxes his grip on my throat just a tad, and I bend down and
pick up the nitrogen, and I say, 'What about Europe, Sam?
I mean, ain't you interested in any other countries at all?' But
that was a dumb question, because now he's screaming at me
like it suddenly hits him the world is my fault – 'We're the only
country! What do we need these other countries for! If they
didn't exist, we wouldn't have to be the rest of the lousy
fucking world's goddam policeman!' I wanted to say, 'Sam, it's
not that you're wrong – it's just that you're so ugly.'

CARL *finishes his beer, surveys the dawn with pleasure.*

I think God was making love when he created the prairie. The
way it kisses the sky in all the right places. And the sweet
fragrance of a fertilized dawn. Nitrates swimming in back of
your skull. Nope – there ain't nothing like an outdoor fourth of
July fuck at 4 a.m.

Pause.

You know what we need? We should get ourselves our own
private nigger, out there on the horizon. Playing some cool jazz
on a muted flugelhorn. Soft tone like a slow blow job and silk
handkerchiefs floating to the ground. Yeah.

Beat. CARL *stands, pulls up his jeans.*

You want some breakfast? You wanna eat some bacon
together? Speciality of the house. Grew it with my own hands.
Killed and cured.

Pause.

So. The Independence Day fuck. How was it for you, mom?
Was it nice? Are you happy?

TWO

ill wind

Shreveport Farm. 6 a.m. RUTH *alone in the cornfield.*

RUTH. The world
    Think about it
    You cry
    If you
    Think about the world
    If you
    Think about it
    If you let it
    Enter your mind
    You cry
    Daniel?
    Daniel?
    Can you hear my heart?

Tornado. Wind rips at her. She's thrown into the air. CARL*'s thrown on by the wind. He's trying to reach* RUTH.

CARL. Here it comes – !

They stand together against the wind.

RUTH. Whoooooo – ! Look at that thing, Carl – !

CARL. Get the fuck outta this, mom – !

RUTH. Gotta be two hundred feet high, whoooooo – !

CARL. Gonna fucking die out here – !

RUTH. I can see you, Satan! You can take my heart, but you're not touching my home – !

CARL. Gonna be picking our pieces up in Alaska –

RUTH. This is our home, Satan – !

CARL. Oh God –

RUTH. Our land! The life that we lead – !

CARL. We gotta get in the cellar, mom, and I mean now – !

CARL *tries to drag* RUTH *away. She resists, defying the storm.*

RUTH. You just hold onto my skirt, Carl! We're gonna look Satan in the eye, the black hole right in his eye – !

CARL. Are you outta your mind? You think I'm gonna stay out here and die of bad weather? It's embarrassing – !

Great black shadow. The tornado upon them.

RUTH. Here it comes, Carl! I can see his horns – !

CARL *cowers, holding onto* RUTH. *Howling wind. Thunder.*
CARL *and* RUTH *are swept off their feet. They fly.*

KRISTIN's *theme. She appears on distant horizon. She dances,
her hands describing intricate patterns of flight and delicacy in
the air, punctuated with moments of gestural violence.*

Elsewhere, ANDREW *appears. He's on a ship. A storm in the
middle of the Atlantic. He's a Highlander, in tartan, madly
wielding a pair of garden shears, drunk on the storm. The
storm rages.*

ANDREW. This is the way the world ends – a mad wind around
ma kilt! Aye, the quivering, shuddering world, come on, blow!
Blow! Ah love a storm! Ah love the wind in ma silver teeth, the
savage sea in ma hair, the savage sea's mad head pounding in
ma head! And all your wailing creatures in ma mouth –
y'cannae scare me! Whooooaagh – !

ANDREW's *thrown off his feet. Sheet lightning.* RUTH *and*
CARL *staggering to save themselves. Prevented by a large
table tumbling out of the sky and crashing into the ground.*

RUTH. Whoooooo – !

CARL. Sweet Jesus – !

RUTH. That was me! Whoooooo – !

CARL. Will you shut up with that whooo noise – !

RUTH. It was my prayer, Carl, I saved us both – !

CARL. What is that – ?

RUTH. It's the Devil's altar – !

CARL. It's the dining room table –

RUTH. He wanted us, laid out across his altar like a sacrifice, but I
stopped him – !

CARL. It's the fucking dining room table, mom – !

CARL *crawling for sanctuary.*

RUTH. Where are you going – ?

CARL. Getting under the dining room table – !

RUTH. You chicken-shit – ! Open your heart to the elements, boy!

CARL. You gotta be kidding! Whaddya think I am, a fish – ?

CARL *hides under the table.* RUTH *whirls round and round, a
crazed rain-dance.* ANDREW *lurches to his feet, brandishing
shears like a sword.*

ANDREW. Do that again, y'bastard! Blow your man down, would you? Ma shears will have your eyes out, ma shears are a mighty brigand's broad sword! Ask me who ah am – Rob bloody Roy, correct! Lick ma claymore – !

He bursts defiantly into song – 'Road to the Isles'.

'The far Cuilins are pulling me away,
As step ah with ma crummach to the road – '

RUTH *collapsing in dead faint.*

'The far Cuilins are putting love on me,
As step ah with the sunlight for ma load – '

CARL (*overlapping*): Mom – ? Get up, mom – ! If you think I'm coming out there, you got another think coming! You hear me? I'm not coming out – !

ANDREW (*overlapping*): What can you do to me, anyway? What's left, eh? What part of ma soul has no' been violated by your Princes, Earls and Dukes – !

CARL (*overlapping*): You can't live without me. Without me you can't even begin to exist –

ANDREW (*overlapping*): Can you hear me howling? The last song of the gardening clan – !

CARL (*overlapping*): Son of a bitch –

CARL *crawling out after* RUTH. ANDREW *singing again.*

ANDREW. 'Sure by Tummel and Loch Rannach and Lochaber
        ah will go,
By heather tracks with heaven in their wiles,
If it's thinking in your inner heart, braggarts in ma step,
You've never smelt the tangle of the Isles – '

CARL *holding* RUTH *in his lap.* ANDREW *enchanted by figure of* KRISTIN *on horizon.*

CARL (*overlapping*): You better not be dead. I'm warning you. I'm the one who oils your ukelele, lady, don't you forget that –

ANDREW. Is she waving at me? You waving at me, woman? Ah'm coming, don't you fret. Ah'm coming to your hearth, America, dragging maself to your house. Ah'm away to the glorious Clan MacAlpine Mountains of Nevada, here ah come – !

Sings once more.

'It's by shiel water, the track is to the West – '

Final clap of thunder. ANDREW, CARL *and* RUTH *disappear in flood of lightning.* KRISTIN *alone. Desolate wind, dying.* KRISTIN's *theme dominant. She dances.*

THREE

atlantic depression

Atlantic. Calm after the storm. A 165 year-old man doing ancient Highland dance upon the sea. Frail and beautiful. KRISTIN's theme growing strands of 'Dark Island'. He's an old crofter.

ANDREW there. The ship approaching New York Harbour.

OLD MAN. A cauld comin' we had of it
  Aye, bloody freezin'
  A dark journey from a dark island
  across a dark sea
  Canada-bound, America-chained
  Nova Scotia, New-found-land
  Hills o' the free
  But no' our hills
  We listened from the greasy belly
  o' the Stornoway steamer
  to the occasional cormorant
  Sometimes seven hundred
  packed in like pilchards
  Three in twenty
  stowed at Stornoway
  never saw the other shore
  The glen weighed anchor
  and the wind whispered 'alone'
  through the fractured remnants
  o' the clan
  Aye
  A cauld comin' we had of it.

  Pause.

ANDREW. Don't dance upon the sea, granda. Ma head's full of sea.

OLD MAN. If we're no' dancing we're cryin'. Ah heard y'singing yir sentimental pap. Just like yir great, great, great grandfather, John MacAlpine. 'Road to the Isles' ma arse. 'Road to Nowhere', more like.

ANDREW. Ah'm crossing the water.

OLD MAN. And what do y'hope to find there, Andrew Lewis MacAlpine? The Land of the Leal?

ANDREW. Ah've had enough. The misery and the drizzle. All the miserable, bloody scenery. All the wee wet towns steeped to the lips in misery.

OLD MAN. Aye but what can y'do? Because tell me laddie, can you farm?

ANDREW. Ah'm a gardener, ah've got ma shears.

OLD MAN. Och, a broad sword indeed.

ANDREW. Ah'm a bloody marvel with ma shears. Look at ma green fingers. Topiary. Got ma bloody diploma. Haven't ah cut the Countess of Sutherland's hedges for ten years? 158,000 acres.

Beat.

OLD MAN. It is the people's land, eh laddie? 'Yir portion make the best of it – The landlords have the rest of it'.

ANDREW. She can have ma country. You're welcome to it, your ladyship, the whole flock of sick sheep. Aye, wave your wand you witch! Change the wilderness into a luxury leisure facility for foreign fucking tourists. Ah couldn't care less. Ah'll crawl no more in your shrubbery, Countess.

Beat.

Ah'm clearing out.

OLD MAN. Och, a tiny wee clearance only. Nobody noticed. His departure was unremarkable.

Beat.

ANDREW. Before ah left ah cut off all the privet-chickens' heads.

OLD MAN. The topiarist's revenge. Aye, well, nothin' changes, does it?

ANDREW. Ah'm sick of eating ma heart out for a lost memory. Ah want no past. No ash on ma shoulders.

OLD MAN. Then it's America you want, all right.

ANDREW. Ah'm following the MacAlpines, Granda. To the Highlands of Nevada. The Land of the Free.

OLD MAN. Oh. Free.

ANDREW (*fishing in his bag*): Ah got a book, Granda.

OLD MAN. Oh guid –

ANDREW. Rosie MacAlpine gave it me for turning her compost. It's about land. And it's about your head as well.

OLD MAN. Yir heid?

ANDREW. She showed me these pictures of the MacAlpine Mountains in Nevada. Look. See? It's great. Pictures and. And hedges look, just waiting for me. And here's a picture of your skull, divided into territories. No' bumps, but, like fields –

OLD MAN. Oh, very nice –

ANDREW. It's brilliant.

He indicates parts of his skull, consulting book.

This part of your skull is agoraphobic. And this is the zone of claustrophobia, just here. See? It's called 'Landscaping the Mind – An Investigation into the Geographical Construction of the Psyche'. It says y'have to seek out the place where your mind fits – the right landscape. Everyone has a special landscape, Granda, where their mind belongs.

Beat.

Well it's interesting. And ah'm going.

OLD MAN. Ah read a book once. Sir Walter Scott. Very busy book, it was. Fillin' our minds with fine truths tauld by an idiot.

Pause.

Do y'think you'll conquer America dressed like that?

ANDREW. Like what?

OLD MAN. Like that.

ANDREW. What do y'mean?

OLD MAN. Why are y'wearin' that abomination?

ANDREW. It's genuine MacAlpine tartan, from the tartan shop. It's traditional, Granda. They like tradition over there –

OLD MAN. A hundred and sixty-five years auld, and ah've never worn anythin' like that in ma life. Take it off, it's a fake, it's a falsehood, it's – fuckin' ridiculous.

ANDREW. But you're still dancing – isn't dancing – ?

OLD MAN. Dancin' is different.

ANDREW. How?

OLD MAN. It loosens the chains a wee bit. Maybe you should learn.

ANDREW. Oh aye, Callum's fucking Ceilidh. No thank you. Ah'll be all right, Granda. Ah got ma shears. Ah got ma book. And ah'm going where the dream begins.

OLD MAN. A pipe-dream, laddie. A bag of air.

ANDREW *sees the lights of New York Harbour. 'Liberty'.*

ANDREW. The Statue, look. The lights on Liberty –

OLD MAN. Oh aye, beautiful. Afloat she is, in a pond of sick green soup. Freedom and vomit.

The OLD MAN *begins to disappear.*

ANDREW. Go away, old man. Leave me alone. Leave me to find ma own road.

OLD MAN. Och, you're a sad young man. Ah cannae help you.

ANDREW. Ah don't need you.

The OLD MAN *has gone.* ANDREW *left wincing at his appearance.*

He's right. What do ah look like? Ah look like a plastic prat from a packet of porridge.

ANDREW *removes the kilt, tossing it into the sea.*

Swallow that.

He looks back across the sea.

Fare thee well, land of scrapie and Scotch myths. Farewell land of Calvin, oatcakes and sulphur. Ma boats are ablaze upon your heather. Ma fish are all fried. Ah'm leaving you – leaving you to the tender caresses of countless Countesses.

FOUR

a woman praying

Manhattan at night. Electric atmosphere of business and hysteria, entertainment and murder.

A POLISH WOMAN *prostrate on sidewalk, arms spread wide. An alley off main street. Nearby an open suitcase displaying trinkets and souvenirs.*

ANDREW *enters, trousered. Notices* WOMAN.

ANDREW. Hey – ? Hey – ? Hey miss – ? You uh – ?

Beat.

Oh Christ –

Pause.

Ah think there's a dead woman here.

Pause.

Hallo – ? There's a dead woman fallen down here. Look. Definitely. A woman –

Pause.

Oh Christ –

Beat.

You're no' from Inverness, are you? Thought ah recognised the posture. Don't worry, eh? Someone'll come by. Maybe someone who knows what the fuck to do.

Pause.

If this was Inverness, ah'd've fucked off by now. Walk on by, that's me.

Pause.

Welcome to New York, eh? Ah hate cities. Don't you hate cities? People laughing for no reason. The air like an emergency. Ah'm a country boy, me. Oh aye. Merle Haggard. Brilliant. Patsy. Connie. Peggy. Hank, Dolly, Don, Tammy. Anon. 'Trad Arr'.

Pause.

Look – you're no' really dead, are you? Because it's hardly fair, is it? – ah've only just got off the boat. Ah'm new in. Need to find ma feet. Learn how to behave and that. Y'know what ah mean – ?

Suddenly a WOMAN *emerges from the shadows.*

WOMAN. Hi.

ANDREW *startled.*

Have you got a cigarette?

ANDREW. Uh – ?

WOMAN. Cigarette.

ANDREW. Ah don't smoke.

WOMAN. That's terrible.

She takes out a pack of cigarettes.

You have a pretty voice.

ANDREW. Do ah?

WOMAN. Yes. Tell me, what is that?

ANDREW. What?

WOMAN. That voice. That language, what is that, is that French?

ANDREW. Uh – no, no, it's uh – Scottish.

She lights a cigarette.

WOMAN. Europe, right?

ANDREW. Ah suppose so, aye –

WOMAN. 'Aye'. I like that. Do you mind if I ask you a question?

ANDREW. No –

WOMAN. Okay. Here's the question.

ANDREW. Right –

WOMAN. What are you doing?

ANDREW. Pardon?

WOMAN. What are you doing?

ANDREW. What am ah – ?

WOMAN. Why are you here?

Beat.

ANDREW. Well – ah'm walking down the street, right? Ah just arrived in your lovely city –

WOMAN. Uh huh –

ANDREW. And ah see this thing, lying in the gutter –

WOMAN. Thing – ?

ANDREW. This woman –

WOMAN. What woman?

ANDREW. That woman.

Beat.

WOMAN. And you thought, 'Oh my God – '

ANDREW. Aye –

WOMAN. You thought, 'Oh my God, what if she's – '

ANDREW. Aye, what if she's –

WOMAN. 'Why doesn't someone – '

ANDREW. Help her –

WOMAN. ' – do something? – '

ANDREW. Do something, aye –

WOMAN. 'Something oughta be done – '

ANDREW. Aye, because all right maybe she is just a –

WOMAN. Yes –

ANDREW. - but she's still a woman –

WOMAN. Right. No, you're absolutely right. Because after all, it could be you down there.

Pause.

ANDREW. Ah just think someone should – do something. Don't you?

WOMAN. Yes. Like what?

ANDREW. Well –

WOMAN. What do you wanna do?

ANDREW. Well –

WOMAN. What?

ANDREW. Ah don't know, ah mean, it's your country.

WOMAN. Yes it is.

Beat.

Do I make you nervous?

ANDREW *nods.*

You're a stranger. And so you feel your strangeness. Welcome to America.

She holds out her hand.

ANDREW. Thanks.

He takes her hand.

WOMAN. The good Samaritan. First moment I saw you, I said, that's what he is. He is a man trying to do good.

She releases his hand.

You planning to stay long?

ANDREW. Well – the rest of ma life, basically.

WOMAN. How long will that be, do you think?

Pause.

ANDREW. Ah think ah'll be on ma way –

WOMAN. Aren't you forgetting something?

ANDREW. What?

WOMAN. The woman.

ANDREW. Oh –

WOMAN. Are you forgetting the woman?

ANDREW. Uh – ah thought ah might, aye.

WOMAN. I thought you wanted to do something for her. Have you changed your mind?

ANDREW. No, ah –

WOMAN. I want you to meet my friend, now. Would you like that?

Suddenly a MAN *emerges from the shadows, close behind* ANDREW.

This is my friend.

Beat.

ANDREW. Hallo.

WOMAN. I know what my friend is thinking.

ANDREW. Do you?

WOMAN. I can read his mind like a map.

ANDREW. What is he thinking?

WOMAN. Well, briefly, he is wondering how it is that a complete stranger – you – can walk into our country, go up to one of our very own vagrants, violate her space, rape her, steal her last remaining trinkets, and then expect us to believe that what you were really doing was demonstrating a uniquely European resource of caring missionary zeal. Am I right?

The man nods.

ANDREW. Oh ma God – ah didn't touch her. She was like that. She's been like that for ages. She's always been like that! Och, look – what's going on, eh? Who are you?

WOMAN. Show him who we are.

The MAN *takes out a gun.*

ANDREW. What's that?

WOMAN. That is a gun.

ANDREW. Oh no. This is no' fair! Ah'm just passing through. All ah want is ma mountains –

WOMAN. I'm sorry. This is my friend's function. He's decided you don't have any altruistic feeling towards her at all, because you're an opportunist fuck.

MAN. Fuck.

ANDREW. Oh God –

WOMAN. But his analysis is flawed, isn't it?

ANDREW. Is it? Aye, it is –

WOMAN. Yes, you see, I believe you are a genuinely caring person –

ANDREW. Aye, right, ah am –

WOMAN. And I am saying – that is your mistake.

Beat.

ANDREW. Mistake.

WOMAN. That is your failing.

Beat.

Do you read the National Geographic?

ANDREW. For fuck's sake, he's pointing a – !

WOMAN. Shut up. I read in the National Geographic that the world is over-populated by eighty per cent. I tell you, I saw that statistic and I said, 'Shit, man, if that's your problem, just go drop the bomb on Iowa or something'. But the trouble is, you drop the bomb on Iowa, who's gonna notice?

MAN. No-one in Iowa, that's for certain.

WOMAN. Right. So we have to enable something else to happen, for the sake of the world. We have to start cleaning up our act. Because the world is screaming.

Beat.

You see what I'm saying?

ANDREW *shakes his head.*

WOMAN. Responsibility. I take it. He takes it. Now you take it. Give him the gun.

MAN *puts the gun into* ANDREW's *hand.*

ANDREW. You're no' going to – ?

WOMAN. Kill you? Kill you? We just gave you the gun. You know, I'm willing to bet he's never terminated a life.

ANDREW. What – ?

WOMAN. We're not gonna kill you. You're gonna kill her.

Beat.

ANDREW. Wait a minute –

WOMAN. Listen, you think the world cares if you care? You think the planet gives a shit? The planet doesn't give a shit. The planet's saying 'What's he gonna do for me?' Because the thing about people who 'care' is they don't do dick. These mother-fucking 'care-takers' are the biggest non-doers of dick in the world. You wanna be a non-doer of dick all your life, you go back where the hell you came from. The only question is what are we gonna do? What are we gonna do about that eighty per cent? Are we gonna take responsibility? Are we gonna participate? Are you willing to participate in the world?

ANDREW. Aye – ! Ah mean, no – ! No' like this – ! Ah mean, for God's sake – look, ah've got ma shears, ah'm ready to participate, just give me a hedge and ah'll participate –

WOMAN. Listen to me. You can do this. You say you wanna do something. You wanna do good. This is good. Do it.

ANDREW. But –

WOMAN. She won't feel a thing. After all, what is she – ?

MAN. Dog food –

WOMAN. Dog food is what she is. You'll be doing her a favour –

ANDREW. No but wait –

WOMAN. The world is waiting –

MAN. Heal the world, fuck –

ANDREW. No –

WOMAN. Do it!

> *Pause.* ANDREW *trembling helplessly. He points the gun at the prostrate* WOMAN. *Turns his head away. Prostrate* WOMAN *suddenly sits up, coughing.* ANDREW *comes to.*

ANDREW. Aagh! God! God! Ah almost did it! Fuck! Fuck! What am ah doing! You made me, it was you! You nearly made me do it! Ah thought she was dead, and you wanted me to kill her – !

WOMAN. Were you dead?

> *She is a Polish emigrant, retaining her accent.*

POLE. No, I –

ANDREW. You were dead!

> MAN *takes step.*

What do you want!

MAN. My gun –

> ANDREW *brandishing gun.*

ANDREW. Fuck off!

> WOMAN *moves.*

And you! Go on! Ah swear ah'll shoot! Ah'll shoot both of you!

WOMAN. You think we can't find some other bum? You think there isn't a bum lying on the very next sidewalk just waiting to be terminated?

ANDREW. Please – don't make me – ! Just – piss – off.

Pause.

WOMAN. Okay. Okay, you win.

WOMAN *and* MAN *retreat and exit. Pause.*

POLE. You save my life. No-one ever do this for me. I am flattered.

ANDREW. Jesus Christ. Ma very first American and she tries to force me to shoot a fucking tramp.

POLE. Excuse me, but I am not a tramp. I am in sales.

She indicates suitcase.

You buy trinket? Trinket from all over Europe. Everything a dollar. Polish doll for all your children –

ANDREW. What were you doing down there? You scared the life out of me –

POLE. I am praying. But then I fall asleep –

ANDREW. Praying – ?

POLE. Of course. In Krakow we got to the fields and lay down on our tummies with our arms out, so. This is how we pray. It is my birthday tomorrow. In Krakow I am hairdresser. But no-one in Poland tell me why I exist. So I have ten years in New York now. I am extremely happy to be free. I am bursting my butt.

Beat.

ANDREW. Ah've got to get out of here. Where's the country? Which way's the countryside – ?

POLE. Countryside – ?

ANDREW. Aye, you know – Nevada. The mountains –

POLE. Nevada?

She whistles through her teeth.

POLE. You don't want to go. Stay with me. We go into business together.

ANDREW. Look, ah'm sorry, all right. Just – which way?

Beat. She shrugs.

POLE. West. Back onto West 57th Street. Find Columbus Avenue. Don't stop. Cross George Washington Bridge. Keep going for – I think nearly three thousand miles. Then ask.

ANDREW *gives her the gun.*

ANDREW. Here. In case they come back.

POLE. Thank you – for my life. Now I have all I need.

ANDREW. Aye –

He gathers up his bag. Beat.

Ah do care. Ah do care, right?

He takes out his wallet. Removes a wad of cash.

Here. You can have it. Och, have it all.

POLE. But it is everything –

ANDREW. Ah'll be fine, don't worry about me –

POLE. No, I cannot, it is too much –

ANDREW. Aye, you can.

He presses the money into her hands. He goes. Pause. She counts the money. WOMAN and MAN enter. Beat. POLE fires gun at them. It's a water-pistol.

WOMAN. Okay, you dumb polack, give me the squirt-gun.

POLE *tosses gun to her.*

How much?

POLE. I count three hundred dollar –

WOMAN *takes money.*

WOMAN. These fucking European tourists, they come over here – no offence, Polly –

POLE. None taken –

MAN. Great days –

WOMAN. You call three hundred bucks 'great days'? Look at this. We can get a fucking shoe-shine with this. He say where he was heading?

POLE. Nevada.

MAN. Nevada – ?

WOMAN. God. He hasn't got a prayer.

MAN. Nevada. Poor guy.

WOMAN *starts to split the money between them.*

FIVE

eau de cologne

Hot afternoon in Reno. KRISTIN*'s apartment.* KRISTIN *by the window waving a decorative fan across her face. Her other hand moving delicately, like a moth in slow motion.*

She takes a bottle of eau de cologne from a table. Applies it liberally to face, neck, breasts. Intense heat.

A woman enters. A WAITRESS. *Sunglasses. Silence.*

WAITRESS. You the woman – ?

> *Pause.*

> You're the woman, right? You do the thing. The hand thing. The thing with your hands –

> *Pause. Takes off her sunglasses. Her face is red and bruised on one side.*

> You – read my palms. You do something – for me.

> *Pause.*

> I can't – I can't stand it – any more.

> *Pause.*

> They said you could help me. Advise me. Show me – what to do. What it is I should do. You can define – the future. What is is, my –

> *Pause.*

> Take my hand? Look at my hand? Will you tell me? What it is I'm doing – to him. You tell me, what can I – ? Where is – the future? You know. You know.

> *Pause.* KRISTIN *goes to touch the woman's face. She flinches.*

KRISTIN. My mother beat me. She expected me to hate her. So that she could forgive herself.

> *Beat.*

> That's why I love her.

> *Pause.*

WAITRESS. I can pay cash.

SIX

problem in paradise

Shreveport Farm. 9 a.m. Aftermath. RUTH *is standing alone in the cornfield, dirty and battered.* CARL *is out in the yard, washing. Bowl of water, towel. Dunks his head in the bowl. Throws his head back. Pause. He looks at* RUTH.

CARL. You gonna stand out there all day?

RUTH. I might.

CARL. All fucking day?

RUTH. I might.

Silence.

CARL. Delphine Hirschenbaum called. Seems old Sam got caught in the storm. Delphine said he ran out into the yard and a flying tractor wheel practically chopped him in half. He's lying in Mercy Hospital in Des Moines joined together by these tubes. Can you imagine? He's in two halves. Delphine sounded terrible. She's all worried in case her health premium's about to double on account of them keeping him in separate beds. So I guess we can count ourselves lucky. I mean, most of the pigs died. And the corn's all laid flatter than grandma's tits. But hell – we got our health, right?

RUTH *goes off towards the house.* CARL *watches her. Pause.*

Hey, did I tell you about the pigs? Damnedest thing, never seen anything like it. Must have been the shock or something. They're just lying there, like they got together and agreed to die, all at the same time. Spooky. Can't be more than five still standing. What do you make of that?

Beat.

I hope to God the insurance covers us for porcine suicide pacts.

RUTH *comes back on carrying an old wind-up gramophone and a record.* CARL *dries himself with his shirt.*

I figure what we do, we get the insurance, reduce on crops and find us an animal with no trace of a religious attitude. Cattle, maybe. Yeah. Old Sam's gonna be selling a whole lot of cows. Let's face it, farming's no life for a man who wakes up consisting of a torso.

RUTH. Was I dead?

CARL. Huh?

RUTH. Was I dead for a moment? Lying in the rain? It felt like I was dead, Carl. For a few seconds –

CARL. What? Listen, I saved your life, and you haven't even thanked me yet –

RUTH. You had your hand on my face, you were stroking my face. But I was way up there, watching it all from another place. Because I was a corpse for a few seconds. Then I slid back –

CARL. Did you hear what I said? I saved –

RUTH. I saved your life, Carl –

CARL. Oh you saved my – ?

RUTH. It was my power shifted the altar.

CARL. Table.

RUTH. Altar.

CARL. Table – forget it.

> CARL *goes to the table, lying on its side amidst the debris. He rights it.*

> Look. It's a table.

RUTH. It's a table now.

CARL. What do you mean, it's a table now?

RUTH. Now it's a table.

CARL. What?

RUTH. But it was an altar then. Things change.

> CARL *stares at* RUTH. *She is cleaning the old gramophone fondly.*

CARL. What is that?

RUTH. It's a memento, Carl.

CARL. A memento? Of what?

RUTH. It's something special for your father.

CARL. I've never seen it.

RUTH. I kept it safe under the bed.

> *Pause.* CARL *turns his attention to the horizon. He studies it. It dawns on him that there is something wrong out there.*

CARL. Hey. Hey, come and look at this. Come here. Stand here.

> RUTH *goes and stands beside* CARL. *He points out.*

> Out there. What do you see?

RUTH. Nothing.

CARL. No, focus on the Hirschenbaum place. Ain't their roof supposed to be level with the top of the great oak over there? Well look! Their place is higher by an inch! What does that tell you?

RUTH *returns to the gramophone.*

What does that tell us, mom?

Beat.

God. We're sinking. Fuck.

CARL *stares around him in disbelief.*

RUTH. Me and your pa, we used to dance together in grandma's front room. Some nights we danced till the moon melted clean away –

CARL. Will you stop stroking that thing and listen to me? Unless the Hirschenbaum place is beginning to levitate, we have got soil creep!

RUTH. Your pa loved Peggy Lee to death –

CARL. Mom! This soil creep is serious shit. It is a mass movement downwards. The earth is moving.

RUTH. But if it is meant to happen –

CARL. What?

RUTH. Things happen that are meant to happen.

CARL. Things change? Things happen? What is this, enlightenment week? I'm telling you, we got a serious problem in paradise –

RUTH. It ain't soil creep, Carl. It's something else.

CARL. 'Something else'?

RUTH. Uh huh –

CARL. 'Something else'? You mind telling me how you have the faintest fucking idea what it is?

RUTH. I can intuit what it is.

CARL. Oh that's good, that's useful, mom. We're probably sitting on top of an enormous cavern, which is right now fixing to swallow us. Did you intuit that?

RUTH. It's not a cavern, Carl. It's a womb.

Beat.

CARL. A womb.

RUTH. That's Old Mother Shreveport down there. Your great grandma. She lay her head against raw nature for us. She was the first. And when she died, she became the earth-womb –

CARL. Excuse me, the what?

RUTH. The earth-womb.

CARL. Earth-womb. Uh huh.

RUTH. And when she breathes the earth moves, and we move with it.

Beat.

CARL. That's – fantastic. No, really.

Beat.

You mind if I make a suggestion?

RUTH. No.

CARL. Good. I suggest, mom, we take the insurance and get the fuck outta here! Because face it, a farm where pigs kill themselves is a pretty poor proposition. But a farm with soil creep is only going one way – down!

RUTH. This is our land, boy. It's promised to us.

CARL. You think I can't leave?

RUTH. You're not going anywhere.

CARL. Watch me! You'll wake up one morning and I won't be in your bed.

RUTH. Where could you go?

Pause.

CARL. Europe.

RUTH. Europe. You don't know anything about Europe, Carl.

CARL. I've been studying Europe for years. I've read all their books. And the crucial fact about Europe at this juncture, is that it's the other fucking side of the world from you.

Beat.

RUTH. There's nothing in Europe. Who in their right mind wants to go to a desert?

Beat.

CARL. Kristin.

Beat.

RUTH. Who?

CARL. Kristin, mom. Your daughter went to a desert.

Pause.

RUTH. You should put your shirt on, Carl. You'll burn up.

RUTH *goes to* CARL. *She stands behind him and lays her hands on him. She caresses his stomach from behind.*

You know, I watched a rabbit once. Got caught in one of your pa's traps? He must have been that desperate to get away, he just pulled and pulled till his leg tore off. He left it behind all bloody in the metal teeth. The next week I saw that rabbit, three legs, sniffing round that trap, he just couldn't stay away. I kept that rabbit's foot for when I went into labour with you. The way I see it, only a dumb animal could dream of doing that to himself.

Pause.

CARL. Well what the fuck. Europe can come to us, right?

RUTH *moves round to face him.*

RUTH. You have got the nicest tits. Sometimes it's like your nipples are watching me. Following me where I go. Look. I got my hands over your eyes.

Her hands rest on him. He gently takes them away.

CARL. Mom. I'm gonna go stare at the pigs for a while.

CARL *exits.*

RUTH. Don't you wanna dance with me?

Pause. RUTH *puts the record on the old gramophone. Winds it up. Lowers the needle onto a scratchy track. Peggy Lee singing 'The Folks who Live on the Hill'.*

A dead man enters. A uniformed private in the marines from 1967. Oozing mud and slime. DANIEL SHREVEPORT, *haunted and shell-shocked.* RUTH *senses him there.*

Daniel? Is that you, Daniel? I knew you'd come.

DANIEL. I'll dance with you, baby. I'll dance with you.

They dance.

SEVEN

fifty five dollars

KRISTIN's *apartment.* KRISTIN *at the table. She take notes. The* WAITRESS *off-stage.*

KRISTIN. Like dirt – ?

WAITRESS (*off*). Yeah like dirt –

KRISTIN. And this is how he –

WAITRESS (*off*). Yeah –

KRISTIN. - makes you feel?

WAITRESS (*off*). Yeah.

KRISTIN. And this is how you feel now?

WAITRESS (*off*). He's just a –

KRISTIN. Like dirt?

WAITRESS (*off*). What?

KRISTIN. Like you were made of dirt?

Beat.

WAITRESS (*off*). Yes.

KRISTIN. Soiled. Good.

The WAITRESS *enters, holding a wet towel to her bruised face.*

WAITRESS. Good?

KRISTIN. Hmmn?

WAITRESS. You said 'good'.

KRISTIN. Did I?

WAITRESS. Yes.

Beat.

KRISTIN. It is good. I mean you are being open. You are being open and that is good. You must speak to me. Whatever you are thinking. Whatever comes.

WAITRESS. Just talk.

KRISTIN. This is how we begin. Okay?

Beat.

WAITRESS. I think I was a little sick in the bathroom.

KRISTIN. Okay.

The WAITRESS *sits opposite* KRISTIN. *Lays the towel on the table.*

WAITRESS. What are you writing? What are you writing down? Can I see?

KRISTIN. No.

WAITRESS. I want to see it.

KRISTIN. You don't need to. It's confidential. It's client confidentiality.

WAITRESS. I'm the client.

KRISTIN. It doesn't matter.

Beat.

I'm simply evolving your profile.

WAITRESS. I thought it would be a straight palm-reading.

KRISTIN. That's not the way I work.

WAITRESS. I didn't expect to have to talk. I mean, I can talk any place. I can talk to myself.

KRISTIN. Yes, do you do that?

WAITRESS. What?

KRISTIN. Talk to yourself?

KRISTIN *makes a note of this. Beat.*

WAITRESS. You haven't once looked at my hands.

KRISTIN. I'm not ready.

WAITRESS. I'm ready. I want you to read my palm. That's why I came. Tell me what's gonna happen. What am I gonna do?

KRISTIN *pours a glass of water from a jug. Pushes it across to the* WAITRESS.

KRISTIN. There's a scientific procedure. I'm not a witch. I'm a scientist. I need your input.

The WAITRESS *sips some water.* KRISTIN *consults a note.*

KRISTIN. So he treats you – he treats you – ?

WAITRESS. He treats me like a piece of shit.

KRISTIN. Yes.

KRISTIN *makes a note.*

And – ?

Pause.

WAITRESS. Okay, you know how you can get a – some guy, comes to your door, a stranger, or they come on to you at the diner because one of your friends said you'd be interested, and all they want is to sell – you know the kinda guy? Before you know it, he's giving you this language thing about how you can get a plot, a plot of land, an opportunity, blah, blah, blah, and he's showing you the map, and it's got a fancy name, right? They give it a fancy name to make it sound really attractive –

KRISTIN. Yes –

WAITRESS. - like 'Highland Spring Rapids' or something –

KRISTIN. Uh huh –

WAITRESS. - and you get there, he's long gone with your money, and it's a piece of shit. It's a dust-bowl.

KRISTIN. Because he lied. That was his job.

WAITRESS. And you believed in him, and you can't understand how you did that –

KRISTIN. But you did –

WAITRESS. But you did.

Beat.

KRISTIN. I see, so he treats you this way, this man, since he found out you weren't the 'Highland Spring Rapids' he expected to find. You disappoint him, so he –

WAITRESS. No, fuck that, I went to him, the son of a bitch, thinking he was the 'Highland Spring Rapids', Jesus.

KRISTIN. You think I'm mistaken?

WAITRESS. Yes.

KRISTIN *makes a note.*

KRISTIN. You're doing very well.

Beat.

WAITRESS. One time, right? You writing? He came into the bathroom. I was kinda – touching myself, bored outta my fucking skull –

KRISTIN. Masturbating.

WAITRESS. Excuse me?

KRISTIN. You were masturbating?

Beat.

WAITRESS. Yeah. And you know what he says to me? he says, 'You want me to do that?' Like I was vacuuming the carpet, and he wanted to take over and do the job properly. So I say to him, 'I don't need you, Francis'. And he says, 'Well baby' – he calls me 'baby', makes me wanna throw up – 'Well baby, that is rightly my territory'. Just like that. 'Rightly my territory'. You got that down? Those are three words I want you to have.

KRISTIN *making notes.*

KRISTIN. Good.

The WAITRESS *takes a drink of water.*

WAITRESS. Can I ask you a question? Is that allowed?

KRISTIN *looks up. Beat.*

KRISTIN. Yes.

WAITRESS. Have you got a man?

KRISTIN. A man?

WAITRESS. Yes, you know, a man. Have you got a man?

KRISTIN. You need to know this. I understand.

WAITRESS. Do you? You're waiting for something special, right? You think maybe the 'Highland Spring Rapids' is gonna come to you, right?

Beat.

KRISTIN. Actually we got a cemetery outside Des Moines called 'Glenview'. You could say I'm waiting for a man called 'Glenview Cemetery'.

Beat.

WAITRESS. Is that where you're from? Iowa?

KRISTIN. A little town called Epiphany.

WAITRESS. Epiphany? That's pretty. You leave a place called Epiphany and come to *Reno?* What are you running away from?

Pause.

I dunno. Seems like I've been heading West all my life. Pretty soon I'm gonna run outta land.

Beat.

I guess I always wanted to travel. I was gonna be an airline stewardess? But I had spots back then so I didn't even make it past the facial appearance counsellor.

Pause.

There just – doesn't seem to be a place for me. Not anywhere.

Pause.

He says there's a job waiting for him in Houston. Can you believe that? He wants me to go to Texas with him. I said, 'Are you kidding? Even I'm not that dumb'.

KRISTIN *is taking notes.*

KRISTIN. You said no.

WAITRESS (*nodding*): He broke my nose.

Beat.

You think I should try my luck in Iowa? Is that what's written down for me? Give me a destination. Excuse me. Hey. I'm talking to you.

KRISTIN *looks up at the* WAITRESS.

Give me a destination.

KRISTIN. You are where you live.

WAITRESS. 'You are where you live'? I don't 'live' anywhere. What does that make me?

Pause.

Your mother beat you. Is that why you left?

KRISTIN *glances at her watch.*

Is that why you left?

Beat.

KRISTIN. My father killed himself.

WAITRESS. Oh?

KRISTIN. Fifteen years ago. Then I had a child. She died.

Beat.

I guess I didn't want to be around that much death.

WAITRESS. You ever going back?

KRISTIN. Oh you know when you leave the place where you're from, you'll have to go back there one day, to face it.

WAITRESS. Why?

KRISTIN. Just to face it. The question is – where do you belong?

WAITRESS. You tell me.

KRISTIN. I will.

WAITRESS. You will?

KRISTIN. Yes.

Beat. KRISTIN *turns back to an earlier note.*

Tuna?

WAITRESS. What?

KRISTIN. You mentioned something earlier, about tuna –

Beat.

I think we should pursue that.

WAITRESS. It was just a –

KRISTIN. Is it something to do with Frank?

WAITRESS. Yeah –

KRISTIN. Let's pursue it –

WAITRESS. But it's stupid –

KRISTIN. No, it isn't. Continue, please.

Pause.

WAITRESS. Well – you ever studied the serving suggestions they put on cans these days? You pick up a can of tuna and there's a picture on the side what to do with it. And the suggestion is, right? You take the tuna out of the can and you put it on a plate. That's it. That's the serving suggestion right there. Put the tuna on a plate. So anyway, I got to imagining one day my own suggestion –

KRISTIN. Uh huh –

WAITRESS. What I do is, I take the tuna out of the can and put it on a plate –

KRISTIN. Right –

WAITRESS. Then I go to Francis –

KRISTIN. Is he in the bathroom?

WAITRESS. I don't think that's –

KRISTIN. He's in the bathroom, jerking off.

WAITRESS. No –

KRISTIN. But he could be?

WAITRESS. No. He's asleep.

KRISTIN. Okay. That's okay.

WAITRESS. Okay?

KRISTIN. Yes. Go on.

Beat.

WAITRESS. Well – I start to cram the tuna into his mouth. I stuff it into his mouth, and then his eyes, and then I get a knife, and put it into his nose with the knife, and I keep on doing that until he's choking and blind. Then I get the tuna company come and take a photograph, and they stick the picture of Francis on all their cans. And that's my serving suggestion.

KRISTIN *makes notes, nodding. Pause.*

What? Did I say something? You gonna tell me I said something significant?

KRISTIN. If it proves to be so, yes –

WAITRESS. Oh good, because I'm beginning to think maybe –

KRISTIN. Yes, that's it.

KRISTIN *stops writing. She puts down her pen and moves the notes to one side. Beat.*

Thank you.

WAITRESS. What?

KRISTIN. Thank you, I have all I need.

WAITRESS. You have all you need?

KRISTIN. Yes. Give me your hands.

Beat.

Give me your hands please.

WAITRESS *holds out her hands.* KRISTIN *takes them in hers. Selects one. Studies the palm in silence.*

KRISTIN. The Influence Line meets the Mount of Apollo.

WAITRESS. Is that bad?

KRISTIN. It's indicative. A love affair is the primary causal factor in your domestic anxiety.

WAITRESS. That's for sure –

KRISTIN. You're afraid of Frank.

WAITRESS. Of course I am, you think I'm stupid?

KRISTIN. No you are not stupid. That doesn't appear. Fear is scientifically manifest. But so is obstinacy. And likewise the ability to carry out a plan.

WAITRESS. What plan – ?

KRISTIN. Fine line leaving the main Life line running across the hand towards the Mount of Luna. Scientifically this indicates travel.

Beat.

There are many travel lines ending in crosses. Journeys ending in disappointment.

Beat.

You are trying to go home.

WAITRESS. What – ?

KRISTIN. Your skin is coarse and leathery. You possess an animal directness of expressed instinct. Your instinct for home is strong.

WAITRESS. Yeah, but where is it – ?

KRISTIN. Pointed finger-tips. Poetic dreamer. For you, home is a dream. You try and leave it behind, but it's always there in your mind. Sometimes you have to leave in order to know how to return. You will go home changed. Stronger. And the dream won't seem so bad.

Beat.

The downward curve of the Head line shows a vivid imagination –

WAITRESS. Wait a second –

KRISTIN. Your thumb, however –

Beat.

I have to point out your thumb.

WAITRESS. What about it?

KRISTIN. In conjunction with the spatulate, here, the bulgy termination of the third finger?

WAITRESS. Yeah, what about it?

KRISTIN. This is portentous.

WAITRESS. What does that mean?

KRISTIN. You are going to act. The spatulate indicates that you will free yourself.

WAITRESS. Yeah, but what does that mean for Chrissake?

Pause.

KRISTIN. An over-developed top joint of this design can sometimes – disclose a murderer.

WAITRESS. A murderer?

KRISTIN. One who murders.

WAITRESS. Let me see that –

She snatches her hand away, stares at her thumb.

Is that over-developed?

KRISTIN. It's developed.

Pause.

Listen. All I'm saying to you is – scientifically you have the ability.

Beat.

You can rebirth yourself.

Pause.

Thank you.

Beat.

I'm sorry – it's fifty-five dollars.

WAITRESS *picks up her bag. Looks for money. Has to empty contents of the bag onto the table. She lays a gun on the table absently. She finds a wad of cash. She sees the gun, picks it up slowly.*

WAITRESS. Am I – gonna use this? On him – ?

KRISTIN. You have that ability.

Pause. WAITRESS *puts her things back in her bag. Pushes the cash across the table. She leaves.* KRISTIN *watches her go. Then she tears out the pages she has been scribbling on. She screws them up in a ball. She lights a cigarette. She watches her hand as it begins to move in the smoke above her head.*

EIGHT

a man praying

Abandoned train-halt, middle of Nevada Desert. Distant range of mountains. A PRIEST *standing on an old railroad platform. Extreme heat. The* PRIEST*'s hands tremble. They try to take off and dance like moths. He fights to control them.*

ANDREW *enters, dirty and ragged. Exhausted. Clutching book and shears. He's reading from the book.*

ANDREW. 'It will be – observed – that the zones of apposition and affiliation – are completely assimilated – into the subject skull's – consanguineous zone – '

He feels his skull.

They are.

Searches the landscape. Sees mountains.

There! Ya beauty! Ah've come home – !

He tries to dance a wee jig, almost collapses.

Whoooer – careful. Careful now. You're in the Land of Beulah, behave yourself. Aye! Canaan! Land of the Leal, granda! Och ah wish you were here to see this, it's – it's – it's –

Beat.

Wait a minute. Wait a minute. Where's ma hedges?

Snatches up the book, finds a photograph.

Is that no' a hedge? Is that no' a fucking hedge – ?

He sways, searching the horizon in vain. Sees the PRIEST. *Lurches over to him.*

Excuse me. Sorry. Excuse me, but – you live here, right? Have you no hedges in Nevada – ?

He keels over backwards in a dead faint. The PRIEST *pays no attention. Suddenly he's talking quickly, obsessively, his hands moving, punctuating his speech with strange gestural flights.*

PRIEST. She's in her little room in Reno. She gets a telephone call. There's a man's voice. He's talking to her and he says – 'I'm the priest across the street and I'm waving to you now, can you see me? My faith is locked in your fists. My prayers are the sounds of poison. I want you to hold my hands, because the language of Jesus is love, the Jesus of language is love, the love of language is Jesus, the love of Jesus is language – the love of Jesus is language.' And she is watching him. And he says, 'I love – I love the way you use that fan on your face, is that a Japanese fan?' And she is smiling at him. And he says, 'I ju – I ju – I just wanted, wanted to say that. I'm not trying to convert you or anything, you're free to do what you want, you can put the telephone down, don't put the telephone down, hallo? You still there? You can put the 'phone down now if you wa – if you wa – if you want. Un – un – un – unless you want to meet me. And I won't come on to you, we can just talk, we can just talk language, I can just sit and answer questions, and you can hold,

you can hold, you can hold my hands. Do you have any
questions?' And she says, and she says – 'Shall I come over to
your home?'

Pause. ANDREW *has come round.*

ANDREW. Okay – okay, look – ah'm sorry to bother you, but –
those mountains – those are ma mountains. Aren't they? Ah
mean, ah'm no' lost, am ah? This is the place, and those are the
Clan MacAlpine Mountains. Aren't they? So just tell me – just
tell me one thing – where's all ma hedges? Where's ma
gardens? What have you done – ?

The PRIEST *is still, distant.*

PRIEST. Shoshone.

ANDREW. Pardon?

PRIEST. Shoshone.

ANDREW. What does that mean?

PRIEST. They are the Shoshone Mountains.

Beat.

ANDREW. Eh? No, no, no, no, no, look –

ANDREW *thrusts the top of his head at the* PRIEST.

Look at that! What does that say?

He finds a page in his book, jabbing at it.

ANDREW. And here, look – it says in ma book, in ma photograph,
MacAlpine, MacAlpine Mountains – look – !

PRIEST. They changed the name.

ANDREW. What – ?

PRIEST. They're totally uninhabitable. So we changed the name
and gave them to the Shoshone.

ANDREW. Listen you, ah've begged and scraped and crawled ma
way across the crud of your country to see this. To see those
mountains, and for what? For you to tell me you've gone and
bloody given them away? Who the fuck to?

The PRIEST *removes his clothes, leaving only his dog collar.*

PRIEST. The Indians. It is ecologically just that I make my guilt
manifest upon the atlases of the world –

ANDREW. What about me? What about ma feelings? Did you
think of that? They're our mountains! Ma family's! And you go
and give them to a bunch of boring bloody Indians because you
feel guilty? How could you dispossess me? Ah've come ten

thousand miles, y'bastard! And what Indians, anyway? Ah can't see any bloody Indians! And why is that? Ah'll tell you, because who in their right minds would want to bloody live here – !

He stops dead, realizing what he's saying.

Oh God –

He throws the book to the ground. He stamps on it repeatedly. Finally he kicks it away. Suddenly the PRIEST *is upon him, grabbing him round the neck, locking his head under one arm.*

ANDREW. Aaagh! Sorry, sorry, sorry –

PRIEST. Listen! Listen, she – ! Listen, she – she – she –

ANDREW. She – ?

PRIEST. She – she, she, she, she puts my fi – puts my fi – my fi, my fi, my fi, my –

ANDREW. Fingers – ?

PRIEST. Fingers – my fingers, insi, insi, inside her cu – she, she, she puts inside her cu – inside her cu – her cu, her cu, her cu –

ANDREW *nodding ineffectually.*

These fingers inside her cu – she put this hand inside her – this hand – and it was – beautiful!

The PRIEST *hits* ANDREW *on the nose.*

ANDREW. Aaagh – !

PRIEST. It was beautiful!

He hits ANDREW *again. Lets him go.* ANDREW *drops to the ground, clutching his nose.*

ANDREW. Ow, God – you're meant to be a man of the cloth, y'cunt –

PRIEST *staring rapt at his trembling hands.*

PRIEST. And – and – and then – she takes his hands – she, she holds his hands – and she says – she says – 'Suicide is scientifically indicated. I'm sorry – that'll be fifty-five dollars'.

PRIEST *suddenly strangely calm. Removes dog collar, drops it. He talks quietly, distantly,* ANDREW *forgotten. As he speaks,* ANDREW *picks up the dog collar. Then gathers up the* PRIEST*'s clothes and crawls off.*

PRIEST. So the priest – goes into the desert. Till he finds an old railroad track – in the desert. And he lies down on the railroad track and – he begins to pray – for a train – to come along and –

eventually – a train – does come along but – the priest doesn't know anything about that because – by then – he's fallen asleep – thinking to himself that – the copper-brown taste of blood – in his mouth – where he's tried to bite his tongue in half – reminds him – of Ash Wednesday nickels and dimes – he collects from his flock – upon a silver plate –

The PRIEST *lays down on his stomach across the railroad track. Arms spread wide. A train comes.*

NINE

carousel

Shreveport Farm. 10 a.m. RUTH *and* DANIEL *still dancing. The old gramophone's needle stuck in a groove, ticking and scraping.*

DANIEL. You remember the old carousel we had in the barn? You remember how we used to ride the red horse together – ?

RUTH. You sat behind me, holding me round my thin thirteen-year-old waist.

DANIEL. And then the twins grew up to ride the same red horse when they reached thirteen. Our own carousel. Imagine that –

RUTH *goes to gramophone, lifts the needle off the record.*

RUTH. It all fell apart, Daniel. After you'd gone – the engine just up and died. There was no-one left to maintain it – not the way you could.

Beat.

I found this tucked away in the corner of that new antique place in the mall. You know how I like to buy you a nice present when Independence Day comes around.

DANIEL. It's beautiful.

RUTH. I knew you'd like it.

DANIEL. And Peggy Lee, too.

Pause.

RUTH. It's hard waiting a year just to see your face again.

DANIEL. There's no place like home in July. Seeing the golf course on fire again. And that taste of scorched earth in the air.

RUTH. The weather's been real mean to us this time. Twenty-six tornadoes in Iowa alone. That's an awful lot of wind.

DANIEL. Didn't pa used to say to us – a twister was the Devil, screwing the ass off the world – ?

RUTH. These are the signs, aren't they? Fires and storms? And the pigs, the crops, the shifting ground. Old Mother Shreveport's awake.

DANIEL. 'I saw an angel cast the Devil into the abyss for a thousand years – '

RUTH. ' – But then he must be set loose for a little time – '

Beat.

DANIEL. He's out, Ruth, ain't no doubt about that. He's on his way, all the signs say so. And you've gotta be ready for him.

Pause.

Listen to me, Ruth. When you're called upon to exercise a little eminent domain, your domain better be your own backyard. Not his. Because I've seen his backyard. I've been there. I've been to his door and sat on his stoop. And he's got hills. He's got hills like you never seen before. And that's where he lives.

Beat.

You could spend a lifetime staring up at those Highlands. From Kontum, maybe. Or Khe Sanh. But you never understand it. There's no room for it in your mind. The place is like an animal. Steam coming off it. This huge black mouth breathing fire. And the stench – like something rotten and fresh at the same time. And all the while Satan's squatting like a crow on top of the mountain. Grinning down at you from Dak To.

Pause.

I got lost out there, Ruth. I didn't know what I was any more. We need it all laid out in front of us. Flat. Or else we're lost. So you let the Devil come crawling to you. So you understand the terrain and he don't. And you tell him straight – 'We mean what we say about Communism. We're not gonna give it houseroom'.

Beat.

He comes in the shape of a crow. He likes it up there.

DANIEL *disappears. Silence.* RUTH *looks to the sky.* CARL *enters fast.*

CARL. Mom – ! Mom, you're not gonna believe this –

RUTH. I've been talking to your father.

Beat.

CARL. Great.

Beat.

So happens I've just been having a very interesting
conversation with Mister Willhard. You know, Mister Willhard
Senior of 'Willhard and Willhard'? I called him up? He was
just dying to pass on this fascinating snippet of information –

RUTH. Carl. We got preparations to make –

CARL. No mom, we got more than that – you see Mister Willhard
of 'Willhard and Willhard' assures me there is no record –

RUTH. You got fences to build –

CARL. Will you listen to me? No record of our premium –

RUTH. It doesn't matter –

CARL. No record at all of any premium –

RUTH. You can't insure against the millennium –

CARL. - in the last six months, I mean who does he think he's
dealing, he's surrounded by computers and he has the gall to –
what? What did you say? What was that you said, I missed it.

RUTH. You can't take out insurance against the millennium, Carl.
It's pointless.

Beat.

CARL. Millennium?

Pause.

You went into town last month to pay the premium. Did you
pay the premium? You go every month, you –

Beat.

I watched you go into town. I waved to you from the barn,
remember?

He stops dead.

Where did you purchase the gramophone?

RUTH. Epiphany.

CARL. Uh huh. When did you purchase it?

RUTH. Last month.

CARL. Last month, uh huh.

Beat.

Jesus God Almighty. Have you any idea what this means?
We're wiped out. We just died. My God. What kind of a lunatic

buys a one thousand-year-old stereo system instead of paying their fucking hail insurance? We're poor.

RUTH. We're not poor –

CARL. We just became poor, you moron!

RUTH slaps CARL across the face.

RUTH. We are not poor.

CARL. What the hell are we then, rich? Some kinda nouvelle rich thing exclusively available to farming families who suddenly discover they ain't got a dime – ?

RUTH. We have riches that cannot be quantified in cash terms –

CARL. Name one!

RUTH. Memory.

CARL. Oh she's gonna pay the grocery bills by demonstrating she can remember the last time we ate breakfast – !

RUTH. Our land is rich in two priceless commodities, Carl. The memory of your father is one. And the other is the millennium –

CARL. I don't believe it. We got no insurance. Farmers with food-stamps. What are we gonna do? What are we gonna do – ?

RUTH. We're gonna get ready, Carl. I want you to go choose a pig for dinner. Then you're gonna put up a ring of steel around the place –

CARL. A what – ?

RUTH. Establish a perimeter. Draw the line. You see Carl, there's gonna be a visitation. I think we can expect – guests.

In the distance KRISTIN has appeared. She is dancing. Her hands floating.

CARL. Guests? Who the fuck's gonna come to a farm where everyone just died and joined the All-American Social Rehabilitation Movement? I gotta tell you, mom – what we need here is a plan. And this plan has got to be – amazing. I mean it's got to be miraculous. You understand what I'm saying? Don't, don't answer that, mom. A man can only take so much disappointment.

CARL exits. RUTH goes to the gramophone. Winds it up. Puts on the Peggy Lee song, 'The Folks who Live on the Hill', again. She stands by the gramophone, swaying gently, smiling. She searches the sky. Behind, KRISTIN dances. RUTH kneels down and scrapes up some earth into her hands. She lets it run through her hands. She folds it into her hair. She scrapes up some more and eats it. Then she plasters her face with earth, wetting it with CARL's bowl of water.

Into this picture, ANDREW *crawls. He is heading for Reno. He is on the verge of collapse. He is now dressed in the* PRIEST's *garments and dog collar. In one hand, his shears. He stops. He sees* KRISTIN, *as if in a vision. She watches him. Pause.*

ANDREW. Excuse me, miss – can ah – trouble you – for a wee glass of water?

ANDREW *collapses, unconscious.*

Tableau.

The song plays on as the lights fade out.

PART TWO

TEN

chocolate milkshake

KRISTIN's *bedroom. Late at night.* KRISTIN *making love to* ANDREW. *She's on top of him, enjoying herself intensely.* ANDREW *responding with a mixture of bewilderment and pleasure. When she's finished,* KRISTIN *moves away to the window.* ANDREW *lies dazed. His new clothes lie beside him.*

KRISTIN. So anyway I was watching this man in trouble, out on the lake. I remember the lake had overflowed that year, and I'd gone in up to my ankles. It was thick mud – like one of those high density chocolate milkshakes you can get that just doesn't go anywhere? It wasn't long before all you could see were these two hands reaching up through the mud. The man's hands – the way his hands moved in the air – it was strange. And wonderful.

Beat.

I watched until they were gone, trying to imagine what he looked like, slowly sinking. You know, were his eyes surprised – or grateful? And then I walked back to the farm. And I guess I decided it was really what he wanted to happen. Because life – can be appalling sometimes, can't it?

Pause.

My father often went down to the lake, just to be alone. When the marines sent him home, they said he was suffering from this thing – this thing they called 'Acute Environmental Reaction'? But I knew, I knew all it was, he needed to be by the lake.

Pause.

And then I had my baby girl. Three years later she was dead too.

Beat.

Leukaemia.

Pause.

I was ostracised by the community. She was illegitimate, you see. I was fifteen. Sixteen. When she died, they blamed me – for bringing the disease of tragedy into their lives. So they drove me out.

Pause. She turns to ANDREW.

I'm sorry, I don't know what made me do that. Seems I can't fuck a priest without wanting to confess my life story.

ANDREW *touches the dog collar round his neck tentatively.*

ANDREW. Look – ah think ah should tell you ah'm – ah'm no' a – ah'm no' – exactly a priest.

Beat.

KRISTIN. What do you mean?

ANDREW. Well, uh – ah mean, no' yet – no' yet, ah'm no' – ah mean – ah could be – ah suppose ah could be, if ah – ah will be maybe, but – one day maybe, but – ah'm still – ah'm still, uh –

KRISTIN. Confused – ?

ANDREW. Pretending. No – practising. No, uh – training –

Beat. He hangs his head.

God. Ah don't know what ah'm doing any more.

KRISTIN. Sounds to me like you're doing your novitiate.

ANDREW. Ma what?

KRISTIN. You haven't taken your vows yet. You're still a novice.

ANDREW. Oh aye. A novice –

KRISTIN. Hey. I know what that feels like, believe me. My probationary year in palmistry was a nightmare. Some days I didn't know if I was coming or going.

Beat.

You've been out in the wilderness a long time. Okay, it's the ideal novitiate testing ground. But let's face it, that desert would be enough to disorientate Islamic Jehad. This is just 'Acute Environmental Reaction', that's all it is.

Beat.

ANDREW. Really ah'm – just a gardener.

KRISTIN. No. That's not true. You have a calling now and you can't turn your back on it. I won't let you do that. You have to set your mind to it like a stone. Because atheism – what is that these days? Atheism is incompatible with a free market economy.

Beat.

ANDREW. Do you honestly think ah could be a priest?

KRISTIN. I know you could. After all, you got such a pretty voice. Scottish.

ANDREW. Aye.

KRISTIN. 'Aye'. See? I like that.

ANDREW. Do you?

KRISTIN. Yes, it's quaint.

ANDREW. Oh good –

KRISTIN. 'Aye'. Scotland.

ANDREW. Aye.

KRISTIN. So where is it exactly? In relation to England?

ANDREW. Above it.

Beat.

KRISTIN. What's it like?

ANDREW. What?

KRISTIN. Scotland. What's it like?

Beat.

ANDREW. Dying.

KRISTIN. Of what?

ANDREW. Nostalgia.

Pause.

There was nothing there for me. Nothing ah recogised. Nothing ah believed in. Just cardboard pop-up history.

Beat.

Ah remember once, standing on the sea-front at Mallaig with an old postcard in ma hand. It was a picture of a wee black lassie. She's saying – she's saying to us – 'If ye wear a smilin' face, ye'll find the world a jolly place – ' And at the top there's a caption – 'We Are Not Downhearted at Mallaig'. And ah thought – fuck off. Just fuck off.

KRISTIN. Those little nigger girls can be so cute.

ANDREW. Pardon – ?

KRISTIN. But you got out, that's the main thing –

ANDREW. Eh – ? Aye – aye, ah suppose so –

KRISTIN. No, that was right.

ANDREW. Was it – ?

KRISTIN. Because you never really belonged.

Beat.

We're all trying to get where we belong. That's what we're all doing. That's the whole story, John.

Beat.

John Gabriel. That's such a nice name. Where did you get a name like that?

ANDREW. Uh – it came to me in the desert.

KRISTIN. It's not your real name?

He shakes his head slightly.

What made you change your name?

ANDREW. Ah didn't much care for it any more. Okay?

KRISTIN. Okay, John.

Beat.

You know, I met a fully-fledged priest once. He lived across the street. One day he disappeared.

Beat.

You won't disappear, will you John? Not ever? beause you're my 'Glenview'.

ANDREW. Your what?

KRISTIN. My 'Glenview'.

Beat.

Listen, John. I know you lost a dream out there. But you found something too. A new name. A new set of clothes. A new destination. Have faith, John. You can rebirth yourself.

Pause.

ANDREW. Ah suppose ah'd better start believing in God, then.

KRISTIN. I wouldn't worry too much about that. I think you'll find contemporary theology no longer regards it as a 'sine qua non' of the priesthood.

ANDREW. All ah wanted was a wee garden of ma own. Was that too much to ask?

KRISTIN. You'll have your garden, honey, I promise. We'll have a lovely garden, attached to the vicarage.

Beat.

You can make me so happy, John, can't you see that? Because there's a place I know. It's so beautiful, John. There's a light in people's eyes, a serenity, you can almost touch it. There's grass. Trees. Hedges. It's God's own country. You can build your ministry there. I can help you. And then at night, we can sit out back and watch the corn grow. It's where I belong. It's my home. And I know it can be your home too, if you let it into your heart. Isn't it time we both went home?

She draws close.

There are other dreams, John. I can show you other dreams.

They kiss.

And you wanna know something? I've always wanted to fuck a European guy.

KRISTIN *pushes* ANDREW *gently down, and they begin again.*

ELEVEN

eminent domain

Shreveport Farm. 3 p.m. CARL *alone in the yard beating a pig with a length of metal pipe. Elsewhere a rocking chair. Leaning against it, a shot-gun. Next to it, a sack full of something.*

CARL. Son of a bitch – !

Hits the pig again.

Die, you goddam son of a bitch – !

Hits the pig a last time. Sweating, catching his breath. RUTH *enters carrying a wooden horse from an old carousel.*

RUTH. We got a field out there full of dead pigs, Carl. You mind telling me why you gotta kill one that's still alive?

CARL. Because there ain't no satisfaction in killing a dead pig, mom.

RUTH *sets the wooden horse down by a water trough.* CARL *watches. She finds a cloth.*

What the fuck are you doing with that?

RUTH. Washing it.

CARL. What you wanna go dragging that thing out for? It's ancient history.

RUTH. I'm gonna rub it down.

CARL. Rub it down? Rub me down, why don't you, I'm the one who needs a rub-down –

RUTH. We're gonna paint it, by hand, every horse. You're gonna repair the engine –

CARL. That engine is beyond repair, mom. Like the farm is beyond repair. Like you're beyond repair, mom, you understand what I'm saying – ?

RUTH. We're gonna turn that carousel into a memorial tribute to your father –

CARL. For crying out loud – how many memorial tributes can a man stand? What the fuck is this anyway, a farm or a museum? You gonna get out everything that's past its sell-by date and put it on show? We got one-year-old yoghurts in the fridge. Let's get them out here. People'll probably pay their entire insurance premium just to come and stare at a tray of antique yoghurts.

RUTH. Are you gonna bleed the pig, Carl?

CARL. Yes, I'm gonna bleed the pig.

RUTH. Well bleed it.

CARL. I will bleed it. In my own time.

Beat.

Tell me, mom. When the time comes, you want me to hang you in the barn and collect your blood?

Pause.

Oh God. Come here? Give me a hug?

RUTH. There's a heap of vegetables to prepare –

CARL. No, come on – just a hug –

RUTH. Carrots and potatoes and turnip greens –

CARL. I'm sorry I shouted at you. It was a terrible thing to say. Just let me hold you a while –

Pause. RUTH *drops the cloth. Goes to* CARL. *He holds her.*

That's better. Isn't that better? I wanna climb in your mouth. Slide down your throat. Wrap my arms around your heart –

They start to dance slowly round. RUTH *slides her hand down the front of* CARL's *jeans. He moves against her hand. Neither notice* KRISTIN *enter. She watches them, smiling gently. She takes out a pack of cigarettes, lights one.*

RUTH. I want you to leave plenty of time to fetch your father this year. We don't wanna be fussing over him when we got vegetables to strain, and the cream to whip for the fruit salad –

As they dance round, CARL *sees* KRISTIN.

CARL. Yeah mom –

RUTH. And if anything comes, anything at all tries to infiltrate, we gotta be ready –

CARL. Mom –

RUTH. - to defend ourselves, Carl –

CARL. Mom –

RUTH. What – ?

CARL. Mom.

They stop still. RUTH *looks up at* CARL. CARL'*s staring over her head at* KRISTIN.

RUTH. What is it?

CARL. It's Kristin.

RUTH *tries to whip round to see her, but her hand's still down* CARL'*s jeans.*

RUTH. What?

CARL. Kristin –

RUTH. Let go of my hand –

RUTH *wrenches her hand free, confronts* KRISTIN.

I don't know any Kristin –

She scrambles for her gun, grabbing it from against the rocking chair.

KRISTIN. Hi Carl –

RUTH *points the gun at* KRISTIN.

RUTH. Who is she? What is that?

CARL. Who are you? What are you?

KRISTIN. I'm your twin sister, Carl. Come home after a decade in the wilderness.

CARL. She's my twin sister, mom.

RUTH. You got no sister, boy! That thing's an infiltrator!

CARL. She's come home, after all this time –

KRISTIN. Ain't been a day go by I didn't think of you, momma. Your pretty blue eyes. Your tender hands on my face –

RUTH. Get outta my way, boy! Let me get a clear shot!

CARL. Put the gun down –

RUTH. Your father told me what to do –

CARL. He didn't say shoot his daughter Kristin, did he – ?

KRISTIN. Lorraine.

CARL. Huh?

KRISTIN. I changed my name to Lorraine. I'm not Kristin any more.

CARL. Oh.

Beat.

Hi Lorraine.

KRISTIN. Hi Carl. Long time.

CARL. Pa didn't say shoot Lorraine, mom –

RUTH. Lorraine? Your father would never have had a daughter called Lorraine. Filthy foreign name like that, we're German! Our ancestry is German, that's what we are round here, you only have to examine the bone marrow – !

CARL. Shut up, mom –

RUTH. It's written all over her, Carl, she's an all-American Commie penetration from Peru – !

CARL. Will you shut up – ?

RUTH. We gotta protect our domain – !

CARL. Mom!

RUTH. What!

CARL. Shut the fuck up!

CARL *snatches the gun away from* RUTH, *hands it to* KRISTIN.

RUTH. Tell Lorraine to get the hell off my land.

CARL. No.

RUTH *goes to speak,* CARL *cuts her off.*

No. Sit down.

Pause. RUTH *slowly sits in her rocking chair.*

CARL. I'm sorry, Lorraine. You can see we're in pretty strung out shape here.

KRISTIN. Saw the corn was down.

CARL. Uh huh. Tornado.

RUTH. Millennium.

CARL immediately jabs a finger at RUTH.

CARL. Don't start.

KRISTIN. Gonna bleed a pig, Carl?

CARL. You know me.

Beat.

How is the desert these days?

KRISTIN. Oh. Same. You know.

CARL. I was gonna commit suicide the day you left. But then I thought – what the hell. There's always someone better off than yourself.

KRISTIN. You gonna kiss your sister, Carl? It's good to see you.

Beat.

CARL. I'm gonna kiss Lorraine now, mom.

He goes to kiss KRISTIN. *She turns her head so he has to kiss her on the cheek. He lingers.*

KRISTIN. Carl?

CARL. Yeah?

KRISTIN. I just got married in Reno.

She gives the gun back to him.

CARL. Reno? Hear that, mom? Lorraine just married a guy from Reno.

KRISTIN. He's not from Reno.

CARL. He isn't?

KRISTIN. No. He isn't.

Beat.

He's in the car.

CARL. He's in the car, mom. He's in the goddam car.

RUTH. What's he doing sitting in the car in this heat? He got some kinda disease?

CARL. Mom, that's gotta be the most pathetic thing you ever said. We don't know if he's got a disease or not. He might not have a disease at all, am I right? They only just got married, for Christ's sake. The subject probably hasn't even come up yet.

RUTH. She's bringing a disease back onto this land, and it smells of Satan!

CARL. Mom, sometimes – !

KRISTIN. He's a priest.

CARL. Did you hear that? Did you hear that, mom? Lorraine's brand new husband just happens to be a –

CARL *stops dead.*

KRISTIN. Well he's not fully-fledged.

RUTH. She married a priest?

KRISTIN. Right now I'm helping him through his novitiate.

CARL. He's a quasi-priest?

KRISTIN. He's finding his bearings.

CARL. Hell, half a priest is better than no religion, right mom?

RUTH. It's a trick.

CARL. Mom –

RUTH. Don't you know a con when you hear it?

CARL. Lorraine is not the kind of woman who would lie to her own family –

RUTH. What kind of priest would marry a thing with her record?

KRISTIN. Oh he doesn't really relate to the past, mom. All that personal history stuff? Why, he says it's all excess baggage. He's generous that way.

CARL. Sounds to me like you got yourself one helluva guy, Lorraine.

KRISTIN. You'll like him, Carl.

CARL. Hey, I love him, he's my brother! Fetch him in here, the poor guy must be half-baked by now.

KRISTIN *turns to go. She hesitates.*

KRISTIN. I scrubbed my soul clean, mom. Right down to the bone. My bones are so clean and white now. It's like I boiled them in a great big pot till all the bad meat melted away. I'm different, mom. I went into exile for you. And I changed out there – for the better, you'll see.

She goes off. Pause.

RUTH. You gonna let her waltz back in here like nothing ever happened? What's your father gonna say when he sees the way our defences have been breached?

CARL lays down the gun. He pulls a rope from a pulley mechanism suspended over the doors of a barn. He takes one end of the rope to the pig, ties it round the pig's hind-legs.

CARL. He isn't gonna say anything. He can't speak.

RUTH. And whose fault is that? Who killed him? She killed him –

CARL. She didn't kill him, mom. He drowned himself in the lake.

RUTH. She wanted him dead. From the moment he was born, she wanted him dead.

CARL picks up the gun, goes to RUTH.

CARL. I want you to promise me, you won't go shooting Lorraine's new husband. We can do without a half-dead quasi-priest on our hands. You can stand guard. But that's all. Just – stand guard.

He gives her the gun. He goes to the pig, starts dragging it towards the barn, preparing to hoist it aloft.

RUTH. She's a messenger from hell.

CARL. Mom! You said to expect guests. Well they just got here, so the best thing you could do is think about getting on top of the vegetable situation, okay?

He hauls the pig up by the rope. It swings in front of the barn-doors.

Christ, you'd think a woman with a half-baked priest in her car was entitled to a little generosity of spirit from her own mother –

KRISTIN *enters with* ANDREW. *He's dressed in the priest's black clothes. Dog collar. Clutching shears. Pause.*

KRISTIN. I'd like you both to meet John. This is my twin brother, Carl. And this is momma.

Beat.

ANDREW. Hallo.

Beat.

Ah've heard about you – no' very much.

Pause.

Uh. Farm. Uh. Very nice. Farm – is this. Aye. Big, uh – very big –

KRISTIN. Small.

ANDREW. Pardon?

KRISTIN. It's only small, honey.

ANDREW. Oh, small, aye. Small, smaller, much smaller than uh – but, uh – in its own way, uh – big. Aye, quite big – for its size.

Beat.

KRISTIN. John's from Europe.

CARL. No!

KRISTIN. Yeah, he's an immigrant. Aren't you, honey?

CARL. You hear that, mom? He's from Europe!

ANDREW. Uh – how do you do, Mrs Shreveport –

CARL. Whoer, John! Not too close. Let's give mom a moment to get adjusted. She's never seen a European before. I think she might be better off sitting down. Sit down, mom.

CARL *sits* RUTH *back in her rocking chair.*

It's been one of those days, hasn't it mom?

RUTH *whispers.*

RUTH. It's the crow.

CARL *whispers.*

CARL. I'm warning you.

CARL *strides over to* ANDREW, *hand outstretched.*

CARL. Congratulations, John.

CARL *shakes* ANDREW *by the hand, too firmly for* ANDREW.

Welcome to the family.

ANDREW. Thanks – Carl.

CARL. Say, where did you get an accent like that?

KRISTIN. He's Scottish.

CARL. What does that mean?

KRISTIN. He's from Scotland.

CARL. Really?

He lets go of ANDREW*'s hand.*

CARL. Where is that exactly?

KRISTIN. England, more or less. Right honey?

ANDREW *is flexing his hand.*

ANDREW (*defeated*). Right.

CARL. He's English? I declare! Mom, you listening to this? She's only gone and got herself an Englishman! That's fantastic! I've seen all your films, John. We get all those black and white features from the fifties – ?

He immediately adopts impeccable pinched Celia Johnson-type accent. Fast.

'Are you happy, darling? I wish I was happy. Wouldn't it be wonderful if we were happy? Do you think we'll ever be happy? We'll never be happy darling. Never – ' Hey, where are my fucking manners? Do you wanna beer? You two must have been on the road for days –

KRISTIN. A few days –

CARL. Insalubrious motels, chamber-maids whispering behind their hands about the priest and the pretty woman in chalet nine – and no-one's even offered you a beer. Mom, why don't you go get us all a beer?

Beat.

KRISTIN. I'll go. Fridge still in the same place?

CARL. It's in there somewhere –

KRISTIN *starts to go.* RUTH *is on her feet.*

RUTH. Where are you going?

KRISTIN. I'm going in the house –

RUTH. You're not going anywhere.

KRISTIN. We feel like a beer, mom, that's all –

RUTH. You're not crossing that threshold.

CARL. Oh God –

KRISTIN. I was born in that house.

RUTH. You weren't born in that house.

KRISTIN. Yes I was, mom. Right after Carl. There's no getting away from that fact –

RUTH. You weren't born! We found you, floating on top of the slurry pit.

CARL *almost laughs.* KRISTIN *smiles calmly.* ANDREW *lays down his shears and steps forward.*

ANDREW. Ah love your daughter, Mrs Shreveport. Ah don't want to be the cause of anything. It must be a shock, arriving out of the blue like this, but – ah want you to know that – ah am a man trying to do good. And ah'm trying to find ma place in the world with your daughter. Because she is the first person, Lorraine is the only person, Mrs Shreveport, and – anyway ah love her, and we want your blessing, but – if you don't want us here –

Pause.

CARL. Are you ashamed of yourself now? That's a true man of God talking to you. Go back to your chair.

RUTH *backs away to her chair and sits.* KRISTIN *kisses* ANDREW *quickly.*

KRISTIN. So he said to me, 'Where do you wanna go for your honeymoon?' And I said, 'I wanna go home to my momma's in Epiphany'. And he said, 'Well that's exactly where I want to establish my ministry. A town called Epiphany.'

CARL. That's something else, ain't it mom? Helluva guy. You showed him round the place?

KRISTIN. We drove up to the Little Brown Church in the Vale, didn't we honey?

ANDREW *nods.*

He wanted to soak up some of the spiritual atmosphere.

CARL. I bet he did. So what's your spiritual impression of Iowa, John?

ANDREW. It's – quite flat.

CARL. You bet it's flat. Why, you can practically see for ever out there.

ANDREW. No hills. No mountains –

CARL. Yup –

KRISTIN. I showed you a hill, honey, when we went through Allendorf –

ANDREW. That was more of a slope, Lorraine –

CARL. I don't know why people make such a big thing of a hill, I never could see the fascination myself –

KRISTIN. Mountains ain't what you need now, John. What you need is somewhere you can see the horizon, everywhere you look – so you can get some perspective on your destiny. Okay?

ANDREW. Okay –

CARL. We can give you horizon, John. If there's one thing we got no shortage of, it's horizon.

ANDREW. Aye –

KRISTIN. You just need some time to acclimatize. Before you know it, you'll begin to get a religious sense of where you wanna take root –

CARL. But you can take root right here, John. Can't he, mom?

KRISTIN. Well we did hope we could stay here for a while, didn't we honey?

ANDREW. Aye, if it's no trouble –

KRISTIN. Just till we find a church that needs a man like John –

RUTH *is on her feet, gun aimed at* ANDREW. CARL *sees it coming.*

CARL. Hit the deck – !

They hit the deck. RUTH *fires at* ANDREW *as he takes cover behind the carousel horse. The shot misses.*

ANDREW. Aaaagh – !

RUTH *breaks open the gun.*

KRISTIN. Quick Carl, before she reloads – !

CARL *gets to* RUTH, *snatches the gun away.*

CARL. I told you! I told you, you crazy old coot! You could have killed all of us!

CARL *drops the gun in the water-trough.*

RUTH. It's the crow! Look at him!

ANDREW. She tried to shoot me, Lorraine –

RUTH. It's the Devil dressed as a crow – !

ANDREW. What's she saying – ?

CARL. He's not a crow, mom, he's a human being, just like you – !

ANDREW. Your own mother, Lorraine –

KRISTIN. It's okay now, it's over –

ANDREW. Doesn't she like priests – ?

KRISTIN. She's surprised to see us, that's all –

ANDREW. Oh surprised, is she? What's she like when she's astonished?

RUTH. It's the Devil, he's been let loose – !

CARL. Mom! It's not the fucking Devil, all right? It's a fucking quasi-priest – !

RUTH. Come the millennium and he is loosed on the world for a little time! Your father knows that, everybody knows that, why don't you? Because you're in league with it! She's brought him here, and you're in league with her – !

CARL. Get a hold of yourself!

CARL slaps RUTH across the face. RUTH immediately slaps CARL back, hard.

RUTH. Don't you hit me! Don't you lay a finger on me! Nobody hits me. Nobody hits me ever again.

Pause.

CARL. I'm sorry.

KRISTIN. Leave her, Carl.

CARL. I'm sorry, mom.

CARL puts his arms around her.

I'm not in league with anyone but you. But listen to me now. John is a man of God –

RUTH tries to pull away. CARL holds her.

- yes he is, and you can't go round shooting men of God. He is our guest. And we should try and have a little dignity in front of a guest, shouldn't we?

CARL kisses RUTH on the forehead. Looks round.

Phew, that was close. You okay, boy?

ANDREW. Ah – ah think so, aye –

CARL. Sorry 'bout that. I reckon she's feeling the heat, John. Down here the heat is real wet. Makes a woman unpredictable, you know what I mean?

CARL eases RUTH back into her chair. Beat. He claps his hands together.

Say! You're all staying for dinner, ain't you?

ANDREW. Maybe we should go –

KRISTIN. Don't be silly, honey. We're been looking forward to dinner, haven't we? I've told him all about the family Independence Day dinner.

CARL. Well it's a unique family occasion, John. Only happens once a year, and with Lorraine missing it's been kinda downbeat. But this year we can do it right. What do you say?

ANDREW. Well – if Lorraine says it's –

CARL. All right! How's your fruit salad?

KRISTIN. Oh, still good –

CARL. She cooks a mean fruit salad, John –

ANDREW. Aye, she does.

CARL gives ANDREW a steely glance.

CARL. Hey, I don't suppose you'd consider taking up your usual position, Lorraine?

KRISTIN. What position is that?

CARL. Oh, you know, taking care of that particular area of the dinner.

KRISTIN. What area's that, Carl?

CARL. The cooking.

Beat.

To be honest with you, I don't think it's safe to let mom in the kitchen alone with a pig. I don't think she's up to it this year, you know what I mean? She's a fine woman in many ways, John. But 'intimate' is not the way I'd describe her knowledge of culinary affairs.

KRISTIN. Well it just so happens I've brought all my fruit with me. The car's full of it. We get it all trucked in from the West Coast. I got cherimoya, grenadillo, rambutan, tangelo, longan, loquat, ortanique and – what else, honey?

ANDREW. Uh – kumquats?

KRISTIN. Kumquats.

CARL. My! Well I never heard of any of that stuff, have you mom? Except kumquats. I remember throwing some kumquats away once. See how cosmopolitan my sister's become? You better go fetch the fruit in from the car, though, Lorraine. Weather like this they're liable to assume a strange identity even the West Coast would find mystifying.

KRISTIN. Okay Carl.

KRISTIN starts to go off.

ANDREW. Lorraine? Uh – Lorraine, ah think –

KRISTIN. It's okay, John. I'll only be gone a second. And Carl's here, aren't you Carl?

CARL. I'm here, John.

KRISTIN. See?

KRISTIN *goes off.*

CARL. You got yourself one helluva woman there, John.

ANDREW. Aye, ah know.

Beat. CARL *goes to the sack next to* RUTH*'s chair.* ANDREW *watches.* CARL *up-ends the sack and empties a whole lot of dead crows onto the ground.*

CARL. Mom's been shooting crows all afternoon. Haven't you mom? Best scarecrow I ever had.

Beat.

ANDREW. Maybe she – shouldn't have the gun. For a while, anyway –

CARL. Maybe. Maybe you're right there –

ANDREW. People – shouldn't have guns.

CARL. He's right. He's right, people shouldn't have guns. Least not crazy people like you, mom –

ANDREW. No-one should have guns.

CARL. You're not a Quaker, are you John? We got a tribe of Quakers around here some place. But they're nomadic. Can't get a fix on 'em. Funny people, Quakers.

ANDREW. 'Course ah'm no' a Quaker, ah'm – a Catholic.

But ah still think there shouldn't be any guns.

CARL. Well, that's a strong point of view. That's a European trait, isn't it? Having a strong point of view?

ANDREW. Ah'm no' sure.

CARL. You'll find we tend to be a mite slow on the opinion front. We like to see our ideas drift in on the breeze, so to speak. See, most folks I know would listen to what you had to say just then, and they'd come up to you in the mall the next week, and right outta the blue, they'd say, 'Well, John, if there weren't any guns, how could we kill things?'

Beat.

Have you read Wittgenstein? What do you think of 'Tractatus'? You know, the bit where he says, when you don't know any-thing, you should shut the fuck up. What do you make of that?

ANDREW. Ah've never read it.

CARL. You're from Europe and you've never read Wittgenstein? Why, he's practically a folk-hero round these parts. I've read all his stuff, haven't I mom? Me and mom spend many a pleasant evening curled up on the couch with Wittgenstein and Zane Grey. That's the kinda people we are.

ANDREW. That's – great.

CARL. It is great, isn't it? Family values, you see, John –

KRISTIN *entering with a big box of fruit.* ANDREW *takes it from her.*

Whoa! Has she come prepared or what?

CARL *puts his head in the box to smell the fruit.*

Mmmmmmmnn! You should smell this fruit, mom.

He picks out a strange-looking example.

The things they got on the West Coast these days. John, take the box over to mom so she can smell this.

ANDREW *hesitates. He approaches tentatively. Offers the box.* RUTH *stares at him.* ANDREW *is transfixed.*

Is she prepared? Do you find her prepared, John?

ANDREW *still looking at* RUTH.

ANDREW. Eh?

CARL. Your wife. Does she come prepared?

Beat.

ANDREW. What does that mean?

Beat. ANDREW *breaks* RUTH'*s stare.*

No, what does that mean, please?

KRISTIN. He wants to know am I a good wife to you, John. Isn't that what you want to know, Carl?

Beat.

ANDREW. Aye. She is, Carl.

Pause.

CARL. How you gonna work this thing, John?

ANDREW. What thing?

CARL. This whole marriage thing.

ANDREW. It is working, isn't it Lorraine?

KRISTIN. It's working for me, honey.

ANDREW. See? It's working.

CARL. But it's a scam, right?

ANDREW. A what – ?

CARL. A scam, a con, a deception –

ANDREW. No – a what – ?

CARL. You're married, boy –

ANDREW. Aye, so? So what – ?

CARL. And you wanna become a priest?

ANDREW. With all ma –

He looks to KRISTIN *for help.*

KRISTIN. Selfhood.

ANDREW. Selfhood.

CARL. 'Selfhood'?

ANDREW. Aye. Ah've thought it through, and – ah've decided – it's ma vocation. Isn't it, Lorraine?

KRISTIN. The whole transaction is vocational, honey.

CARL. Well, I don't pretend to know much about it. I mean, we're all Lutheran. A kind of evangelical confessionism founded upon Lutheran fundamentals. But it seems to me, John, there's a question here, and it's this. Are you hoping to obtain some kinda special dispensation from the Pope?

Beat.

ANDREW. The Pope?

CARL. Yeah, you know, the Pope?

ANDREW. No, uh, who? Ah mean, no, wait a minute, what's it got to do with the Pope? He's bloody miles away –

CARL. 'He's bloody miles away'! I love this guy!

KRISTIN. I knew you'd like him –

CARL. Like him? I love him!

ANDREW. Wait –

CARL. This guy doesn't even know who the Pope is!

ANDREW. No, wait – ah do, ah do – wait for me – tell him, Lorraine –

KRISTIN *takes the box from* ANDREW.

CARL. Say, Lorraine, what's your married name? What's this guy's name? What name you given her, John?

Beat.

ANDREW. Gabriel.

CARL. Huh?

KRISTIN. Gabriel.

CARL. No! Lorraine Gabriel?

KRISTIN. Uh huh –

CARL. You taking all this in, mom? This is no ordinary Englishman she's married. No, she's married a motherfucking angel who's never heard of the Pope! It's beautiful, John, what can I say? I think you're gonna make a terrific priest, really I do. Can't lose –

ANDREW *sits down in the dirt, holding his head.*

That's it, John, you sit right down there in the dirt, make yourself at home, boy. I mean it –

ANDREW. Something wrong –

CARL. What's the matter, you got a headache?

KRISTIN. He gets headaches.

CARL. Frankly I'm not surprised –

ANDREW. Something wrong with this place –

CARL. Is the heat getting to him, do you think?

KRISTIN. No, this is one of his landscape headaches, right honey?

ANDREW. Why did you bring me here, Lorraine? Why – ?

KRISTIN. Because it's beautiful here –

ANDREW. But you can see too far – and there's fuck all to see – !

KRISTIN. He's got this geographical mindsickness, same as pa? He'll get over it –

CARL. Well you should take good care of yourself, John. You might find the best place for you is inside the house, locked in Lorraine's old bedroom, with all the curtains tight shut. Right, Lorraine?

CARL *goes to the carousel horse.*

Ever ridden a carousel, John? You remember this old thing, baby?

KRISTIN. Sure. It was real pretty.

CARL *puts a foot on the wooden horse.* RUTH *is on her feet.*

RUTH. Don't you touch that, Carl –

CARL (*mildly*). I'll touch anything I damn please, mom.

He pushes the horse over. RUTH *runs and kneels by it, stroking it.* CARL *picks up* ANDREW's *shears, snipping at the air.*

So what's the story with these cutters, John? It's gotta be something extraordinary, right – ?

ANDREW. No, don't touch ma shears –

KRISTIN. Oh that's my husband's little hobby. Whaddya call that hobby, honey?

ANDREW. Topiary –

CARL. 'Topiary'? What is this 'topiary' thing? Enlighten me. You think your brother-in-law could learn to 'tope'?

ANDREW. It's nothing –

KRISTIN. It's an art.

CARL. Art? You're an artist now?

ANDREW. Ah was a gardener, a fucking gardener, that's all –

CARL. What do you mean, a gardener? You're a regular Renaissance man, John, I can't begin to compete with you –

KRISTIN. He cut every hedge on the outskirts of European civilization. He was directly responsible to a Queen – or what was that thing you said, honey, that title?

ANDREW. Countess.

KRISTIN. Countess, that's right, the Countess of Sutherland –

CARL. Hey, hey, hey, this is too much for me, you telling me he's a member of the Royal Family?

ANDREW. For fuck's sake –

CARL. John! I'm in a daze! I'm in a whirl! How the fuck do you manage it! What a guy!

CARL *is by the pig. He slaps it. It swings back and forth.*

So, John, with all your talents and qualifications, you must know an awful lot about pigs. Am I right?

ANDREW. No.

CARL. Well what do you know about pigs? I hope you know something, because we need an expert.

CARL *catches the swinging pig.*

You see we got quite a problem on the farm. We got a dead pig problem. We have a surfeit of dead pig, in fact. What do you suggest we do about it?

ANDREW. Ah don't know what to do – !

CARL. Well you're an artist, John. Use your imagination.

I thought you Europeans had all the answers. Are you saying you're not a European?

What are you, John? What are you?

Beat.

ANDREW. What am ah, Lorraine? You tell me what ah am. You know. You know – !

CARL. I'm afraid I'm gonna have to confiscate these shears. You see, I don't hold with shears. People shouldn't have shears, John. There shouldn't be any shears.

He drops the shears in the water-trough. ANDREW *helpless.* CARL *goes to* KRISTIN. *She takes fruit from the box. He takes out his pig-knife. Offers it to* KRISTIN. *She cuts a big piece of fruit in half with it, squeezes it into his mouth. He takes some fruit, squeezes it into her mouth.* ANDREW *crawls to the water-trough to retrieve his shears.*

ANDREW. Aye, what is he? A gardener with no' a single blade of grass to his name. Is that no' funny? Are we no' mocked? Show me the page in the Good Book where it says the gardeners are no' funny. Mock the gardeners. Blessed are the gardeners, for they shall have no land. No' a scritchy-scratchy clod of cow-shite, no' a snip-snip-snip of Sutherland hedge, and no land for their fathers. And no land for their fathers' fathers –

Pause.

Look Lorraine. Tears of a poor wee gardener. Last of a putrid clan, clan MacAlpine, the clan that never was –

ANDREW *sits with his shears in his lap. During his speech* CARL *and* KRISTIN *have drawn close, smearing each other in juice and torn lumps of fruit. They lower themselves to the ground.* KRISTIN *takes* CARL's *hands, slides them inside her blouse.* CARL *buries his head between her legs, taking some fruit in there with him.* RUTH *is on her feet, staring at it all.* ANDREW *becomes aware of them, as* KRISTIN *wraps her legs around* CARL's *waist.*

ANDREW. Lorraine? What – what are you doing?

RUTH. You just gonna sit there! She's moving in on him!

ANDREW. Lorraine – ?

KRISTIN (*kissing* CARL). Whaddya want, honey?

ANDREW. What are you doing?

RUTH. He's walking all over you! She's making him do that!

ANDREW. Lorraine – !

RUTH. That's your territory – !

ANDREW. You and me – !

RUTH. That's my territory – !

ANDREW. Me and her, Carl! She's ma wife, you're ma wife, we're married, Mrs Shreveport – !

RUTH. He's stealing your land, boy! He's gonna plant some feeling in that soil, that feeling's gonna germinate, and a disease is gonna grow, all over again, is that what you want? Is that what you want – !

ANDREW *clutches his shears to his chest, hapless.*

ANDREW. Stop – stop it, Carl –

RUTH. You gonna let this happen to me! Do something!

CARL. You're not trying to form a pact with the Devil, are you mom? Not against your own daughter – ?

RUTH. Help me, boy! You gotta stop her!

ANDREW. Lorraine, you shouldn't be doing that! Not with your own brother, Lorraine – !

KRISTIN. Whose brother would you rather I was doing it with?

ANDREW. What – ?

RUTH. Defend yourself! Attack! You gotta exercise eminent domain here!

CARL. How about it, John? You gonna exercise a little eminent domain – ?

CARL *and* KRISTIN *kiss passionately.*

RUTH. Take her away from him! Give him back to me! Go to war, boy!

CARL. Go to war, mom? That's bad advice, haven't we learned anything at all from history? Don't go fighting a land war in a country you don't even begin to understand. Right, John – ?

ANDREW. Lorraine – you said you loved me. Don't you love me – ?

KRISTIN. Love you, John? Of course I love you. In my own way.

ANDREW. You can't do this! What does it mean? What about me? What about God?

He turns to RUTH.

What about God, Mrs Shreveport – ?

Beat.

RUTH. You useless, useless – Communist.

> RUTH *punches* ANDREW *in the stomach with all her might. He never sees it coming. He collapses, pole-axed.* RUTH *goes back to her rocking chair, defeated.* KRISTIN *leaves* CARL, *stands. Pause.* ANDREW *is lying underneath the pig.*

KRISTIN. I want John to be a true member of this family. I want him to be welcomed in the traditional manner, Carl. Just the way pa did it to us when we were babies.

> CARL *gets to his feet, grabbing his pig-knife.*

CARL. Okay! Now you're talking!

> KRISTIN *kneels beside* ANDREW, *cradling his head in her lap. She strokes his hair.* ANDREW *clutches his stomach, dazed.*

KRISTIN. You remember the last time we did this, Carl?

CARL. Huh?

KRISTIN. You must remember the last time we baptized a baby together.

> CARL *is thrown. He hesitates, standing beside the pig.*

What about you, mom? Surely you remember the last time?

> RUTH *is broken. She speaks quietly.*

RUTH. Get out –

> ANDREW *is staring distantly, dazed and lost.*

ANDREW. She cried – in ma arms. Ah felt – sorry for her. And then – ah fell in love. What was ah supposed to do? She told me – her life was – tragic. Tragic – that's what she said, Mrs Shreveport –

KRISTIN. It was tragic, wasn't it mom? Losing your only grandchild that way? I can still see her to this day. Waving at the window of the hospital. Those little hands, fluttering gently in the air like a moth. You remember her waving at us, don't you Carl – ?

CARL (*quietly*). She had her mother's hands.

KRISTIN. And those piercing blue eyes, staring after us as we drove away. She had her father's eyes.

> KRISTIN *and* CARL *staring at one another. Beat.* ANDREW *trying to focus.*

ANDREW. What – ? Oh God – oh ma God, Lorraine – what are you saying? Please. Tell the truth –

KRISTIN. The truth, John? The truth is – something comes along and you deal with it, that's the truth. You deal with it, and then you forget it. Right, Carl? Action and transaction, that's all there is to it. And the only question that matters is what are you capable of doing.

ANDREW. What comes along – ?

KRISTIN. Something comes along. Like a baby.

ANDREW. Your baby – ?

KRISTIN. Yes. Our baby comes along. And our baby starts to get sick. And it's like it hits you then, the facticity of disease hits you, and you realize all of a sudden that something's wrong with the balance of the situation. Something that wasn't wrong becomes wrong overnight. Because tragedy is wrong, isn't it mom – ?

RUTH. Get out. Get back to the slurry pit –

KRISTIN. So then you need to correct the balance. And the first thing you do is you isolate the culpable in your mind. Then you surround that object of blame in your mind, and you exile it. You exile it from your memory. You learn to push it so far out of your memory, you never dream of it coming around again to haunt you.

Pause.

A true member of this family, John, knows exactly how to deal with the past.

Pause.

Come on Carl. What are you waiting for? You've gotta go get pa, and I've got a dinner to cook. Let's do it.

Beat.

CARL. Whatever you say, Lorraine.

CARL holds the pig, and positions it over ANDREW. He takes his pig-knife and slits the pig's throat. The blood gushes out and soaks ANDREW. He climbs unsteadily to his feet.

KRISTIN. Oh John. Don't look like that. It's just a little blood.

Silence. ANDREW begins slowly to dance, echoing the OLD MAN's fragile Highland dance. From a distance, a pipe band playing 'Dark Island', growing closer as he dances.

ANDREW. Watch me
    Watch me, granda
    Can you see me?
    Are you watching?
    Ah'm dancing granda
    Ah'm dancing.

TWELVE

the king of sutherland

Shreveport Farm. 10 p.m. A table in the middle of the yard, laden with the debris of the family Independence Day dinner. Remains of the pig. A huge bowl of fruit salad, half-eaten. Numerous cans of beer. The old gramophone. Dead crows scattered around.

CARL is sitting at the table, head slumped in his arms. He's drunk. At one end of the table, ANDREW sitting, frozen, caked in dried blood. At the other end of the table, DANIEL SHREVEPORT is sitting. He is a substantially decomposed corpse, exhumed for the occasion, according to the family Independence Day tradition. He is wearing a helmet, and dressed in what remains of his marine uniform. Between what's left of his lips, a cigar, which has gone out. ANDREW is clutching his shears to his chest.

RUTH in her rocking chair, staring vacantly. KRISTIN standing alone, a little away from the table. Silence.

Suddenly CARL jerks awake, eyes wild, beer cans and food go flying.

CARL. Hey! Hey, I just had an amazing idea! It came to me in a
    blinding flash, a moment of epiphany! Listen, mom – I got the
    plan! What we do, see, what we do – we turn the whole place,
    the whole fucking farm – into – a fun-fair! Yeah! The finest, the
    biggest, and the best goddam fun-fair in the entire State! And
    right, right in the middle, right dead centre of the fun-fair, going
    round and round, we erect 'The Daniel Shreveport Memorial
    Carousel', right pa? Your cigar's gone out, pa. And then, and
    then what we have – is a throne – yeah, a throne – and sitting
    on this throne, waving at everybody, you know, like they do,
    we got John, our very own member of the Royal Family – and
    he says 'Hallo' to all the little people as they come in through
    the gate! Is that a fucking plan or what!

He goes to DANIEL and removes the tin helmet, staggering over behind ANDREW.

Okay – okay, everybody – here we go –

He steadies himself.

On this, on this – you listening to this, mom? Pay attention now. On this beautiful – beautiful – blue night – in the heart of the West – I hereby crown you – King – King John – King of all you survey – and all who sail in her –

He ceremoniously lowers the tin helmet onto ANDREW's *head.*

Ladies and gentlemen – ladies – may I present – King John of – Sutherland – Sutherland Leisure Facility and Family Fun-Fair, in the great State of Iowa –

CARL *staggers round and sits on the table right in front of* ANDREW, *his feet on* ANDREW's *lap.*

Excuse me, your majesty –

He leans forward conspiratorially towards ANDREW.

John. I wanna tell you something, now. Do you mind? Something you Europeans never seem to understand. In this life – you gotta learn – to shovel all the shit behind you, as you go. Do you know what I'm saying? She knows. Kristin knows. Because life, John! Life – is all about disintegration. Things fall apart. Things sink. It's the Second Law of Thermodynamics, John. And there isn't a fucking thing you can do about it –

Beat. CARL *collapses backwards across the table, dead to the world. In the silence that follows,* RUTH *leaves her rocking chair.*

RUTH. Am I too young to get married, grandma?

KRISTIN. 'You falling in love again, baby?'

KRISTIN *assumes the role of* RUTH's *grandmother – old mother Shreveport.* RUTH *is like a child.*

RUTH. Oh grandma, he's the most beautiful boy in Iowa, I watched him touch his hair in church like this –

KRISTIN *goes to the table. She takes pieces of fruit out of the bowl and plasters* CARL's *head and face with them.* CARL *is unconscious throughout.* KRISTIN *crams fruit into his mouth, his eyes, his ears, his nose, punctuating her great grandmother's words.*

RUTH. Grandma, do you think the boy will notice the way my eyes shine whenever he's near?

KRISTIN. 'Do you see how the Summer sun catches you pa's pig-knife and makes it shimmer? Well that's how your pretty blue eyes shine'.

RUTH. Oh Grandma, I just gotta get married.

KRISTIN. 'Now baby, you only seven years old. You look at my scrawny skin and hold all my experience in your arms a while. Seems to me I lived to see a thousand years of progress. From the horseless carriage, through two world wars, and the first man to walk on the moon. So you listen to me, baby. The times in which we live are not what matter. It's not being poor, it's not about being poor, it's about being patient, and waiting, and learning to live in harmony with the prairie, and being good, and respecting those who care about you, like your ma and me, and loving us back with all your soul.'

RUTH. But grandma – you know – ma hits me real hard. Real hard.

KRISTIN. 'I know baby, but your ma doesn't really mean to hurt you. She just gets kinda tired and the Devil inside her starts throwing his weight around like some drunken bum trying to find his way outta Nebraska. And the Bible says people are always gonna suffer for no reason, so you see it ain't really her at all. When you got children and you're looking after the farm, you'll know just what you have to do to get by. She really loves you, baby. Everybody loves you. Everybody in the whole world loves you, baby'.

Silence. KRISTIN has finished with CARL. She goes to RUTH and kisses her on the lips. RUTH is still. KRISTIN goes to the old gramophone. She winds it up and puts on the Peggy Lee record. She finds a track and lowers the needle. 'Is That All There Is' begins to play softly. KRISTIN goes to RUTH's rocking chair and calmly lowers herself into it. Pause.

KRISTIN. You're one of us now, John. This is truly where you belong. We'll be here for a thousand years. Until all the angels come.

Pause. ANDREW speaks with difficulty.

ANDREW. The world. The world, Lorraine –

KRISTIN. What about the world, John?

ANDREW. It can't – work. Can it? No' like this – ?

KRISTIN. It's working for me, honey.

Beat.

It's a wonderful world.

KRISTIN *rocks gently in the chair. Pause.*

ANDREW. There was a man
and he was mad
and he ran up the steeple
and there he cut his nose off
and flung it at the people

Pause. ANDREW *slowly takes up his shears and cuts his nose off.
the Peggy Lee song swells.* RUTH *dances.*

The End.

STAR-GAZY PIE AND SAUERKRAUT

In memory of Bethia and Matthew
and for Nance, their mother

Note

In 1991 I was commissioned to write a play called *The Shaming of Bright Millar* which was produced by Contact Theatre in Manchester. It received fifteen performances in May of that year. Brigid Larmour directed the play with intelligence, sensitivity and skill, bringing together a great company of actors: Laura Bratton, Paul Brightwell, Joan Heal, Vikki Lennox, Robin Soans and Chris Wilkinson. The designer was Richard Aylwin. I am grateful to everyone involved in the earlier play.

Long after the production I found myself returning to the script, feeling that the world of the play could be explored much further: introducing new characters and new scenes, making cuts and revisions, and yet preserving some of the original play. The Royal Court encouraged me in this process, giving me the incentive to develop the script through several drafts. But without the intellectual clarity, practical criticism and inspired suggestions of both Rob Soans in the earlier stages of re-writing, and of Mark Wing-Davey in the latter stages, the resulting script, *Star-Gazy Pie and Sauerkraut*, would have been a much lesser thing altogether.

JAMES STOCK

Manchester, May 1995

Star-Gazy Pie and Sauerkraut was first performed at the Royal
Court Theatre Upstairs, London, on 4 May 1995. The cast was
as follows:

JUDITH / BRACK	Geraldine Alexander
ANNIE / CHYLE	Anita Carey
BILLY / BRIGHT / SICK CHILD / SERVANT	Greg Chisholm
GEORGE / MORELL / DILL	Robin Hooper
KATHLEEN / SECRETARY	Samantha Morton
OTTO	Eivind Rossow
FRANK / HITLER / KEEPER	Robin Soans
MARIA	Bridget Turner

Director Mark Wing-Davey
Designer Claudia Mayer
Sound Designer Paul Arditti

Scenes

Unless otherwise stated, scenes take place on the north coast of Cornwall in 1983.

PART ONE

One – lifebuoy
Two – natrum muriaticum
Three – white horses
Four – painting by numbers (Bavaria, 1925)
Five – slugs
Six – a fiend hid in a cloud (Cornwall, 1808)
Seven – the pity of strangers

PART TWO

Eight – the arithmetic of memory (Berlin, 1940)
Nine – indigestion
Ten – lac caninum
Eleven – a shaming (Cornwall, 1808)
Twelve – more light
Thirteen – the question
Fourteen – urlicht

Note on layout: / marks a point of interruption. Sometimes this entails a character continuing to speak through another's speech; and occasionally it might mean two characters interrupting a third at the same time.

Characters

KATHLEEN TREYARNON (14)
ANNIE TREYARNON – *her mother* (37)
MARIA SCHWENIGER – *her grandmother* (63)
JUDITH SCHWENIGER – *her aunt* (35)
FRANK LUCKETT – *a fisherman* (39)
BILLY LUCKETT – *his son* (14)
GEORGE LUCKETT – *his brother* (45)
ADOLF HITLER
THEODOR MORELL
KATRIN BRACK
OTTO SCHWENIGER
SECRETARY
SERVANT
SICK CHILD
BRIGHT MILLAR
DOCTOR CHYLE
STANLEY DILL, BISHOP OF TRURO
KEEPER

Parts are doubled as follows:
FRANK / HITLER / KEEPER
ANNIE / CHYLE
JUDITH / BRACK
GEORGE / MORELL / DILL
KATHLEEN / SECRETARY
BILLY / BRIGHT / SICK CHILD / SERVANT
OTTO

PART ONE

ONE

lifebuoy

Doctor's surgery in Padstow. Day. BILLY *twisting a stethoscope in his hands.* ANNIE *and* FRANK *there.*

FRANK. He won't look at me.

ANNIE. I know –

FRANK. He's never once looked into my eyes.

ANNIE. Frank, it's normal. It's not you.

FRANK. Well it must be.

ANNIE. You can't take him out of the school –

FRANK. I can –

ANNIE. You can't, / Frank –

FRANK. Why can't I? / He's my son, I can do what I –

ANNIE. Because that's what he's there / for, Frank,

FRANK. But tedn' working –

ANNIE. you can't bring him here, / it isn't

FRANK. Why not – ?

ANNIE. fair, / I'm not

FRANK. What – ?

ANNIE. qualified, it isn't / my field –

FRANK. What – ?

ANNIE. I'm / not –

FRANK. You're a doctor, / aren't you – ?

ANNIE. I'm a G.P. –

FRANK. Yeah –

ANNIE. I'm not an / expert –

FRANK. You're a doctor –

ANNIE. But I can't / do anything for him, it's not my –

FRANK. Why not? What's the matter with you? I'm telling you, / he's not getting any better –

ANNIE. It's up to the school, they know / what they're –

FRANK. The school is shit –

ANNIE. The school is not / shit, Frank –

FRANK. The school is shit, it's not even / real –

ANNIE. It's a special / school –

FRANK. It's not even a real school, it's a fucking mad / house –

ANNIE. You're being / ridiculous –

FRANK. Have you been – ?

ANNIE. No –

FRANK. Christ, you think he's an idiot, don't you? / He's not

ANNIE. No, I –

FRANK. an idiot, he's my son, he's gifted. He's gifted, I've seen it on the telly, / I've read about it –

ANNIE. That's wonderful, / what

FRANK. I've read books –

ANNIE. does your wife say, Frank – ?

FRANK. She's gone, that school, they say his score's still thirty-six. Thirty /six – !

ANNIE. I.Q. – ?

FRANK. No not his fucking / I.Q., where he is

ANNIE. His assessment –

FRANK. on the scale, the fucking 'CARS' thing, / you think

ANNIE. Right –

FRANK. he's thirty-six – ?

ANNIE. Me? I've no / idea –

FRANK. He can draw, he's brilliant, / that's

ANNIE. I know –

FRANK. not thirty fucking six, thirty-six is / for idiots –

ANNIE. I don't know what you want / me to do –

FRANK. What – ?

ANNIE. What is it you want?

Beat.

FRANK. I want you to make him better.

ANNIE. I can't do that.

FRANK. Listen. I've come here because I want you to give him something to / put him right –

ANNIE. What's the point – ?

FRANK. Because thass what you're / meant for.

ANNIE. There's no point coming here, Frank.

FRANK. What? No, look, I'm asking you to help him / thass all –

ANNIE. I can't –

FRANK. No, I'm asking, please, help / him –

ANNIE. There's noth –

FRANK. Help him. Please. Please. Please / help him –

ANNIE. I can't, / Frank –

FRANK. Help him!

Beat.

ANNIE. There's nothing I can do. I'm sorry.

FRANK. Sorry?

ANNIE. Yes.

FRANK. You're sorry?

Pause.

Why idn' there a pill?

ANNIE. I don't know.

FRANK. There should be a pill. One pill. And he's better.

ANNIE. Yes –

FRANK. Don't you think?

ANNIE. Yes.

Beat.

FRANK. You fucking useless kraut.

Pause. ANNIE *goes to* BILLY.

ANNIE. Can I have that, Billy? Please?

BILLY *clutches the stethoscope more tightly.*

Billy? Can you give it to me? What is it, Billy, what have you got? What's it called – ?

FRANK. Leave him –

ANNIE. Do you know what it is? Can you say it? Can you say it, Billy – ?

BILLY *is rocking as his anxiety rises.*

FRANK. Leave him alone, / will you – ?

ANNIE. Try and say it, Billy –

BILLY. Mmm –

ANNIE. Come on –

BILLY. Mmm –

FRANK. You're upsetting him –

ANNIE. Say it, Billy, come on –

BILLY. Mmm –

FRANK. I said you're / upsetting him –

BILLY. S – s – sst –

ANNIE. Yes, go on –

BILLY. Sst – st – ste –

ANNIE. Yes –

BILLY. Ste –

FRANK. Stethoscope. All right?

FRANK *snatches stethoscope away from* BILLY, *thrusts it into* ANNIE*'s hands.*

Fucking stethoscope. Christ.

ANNIE. You see the point is, Frank, what's best for Billy? What's the best thing you can do for him? / It isn't coming to me.

FRANK. I know you. You think if we'd drowned him at birth, or something –

ANNIE. No –

FRANK. Liar. Liar –

ANNIE. How dare you –

FRANK. Oh fuck off. He'd be better off, wouldn't he? Wouldn't he?

FRANK *pulls* BILLY *away. They go.* ANNIE *is still. Pause. She takes out a pack of cigarettes.*

ANNIE. 'Doctor, doctor . . . I feel like a bar of soap.'

Lights a cigarette.

'That's life boy.'

She stands. Smokes the cigarette.

TWO

natrum muriaticum

Fisherman's cottage in Padstow. Night. BILLY *on floor of his bedroom, humming as he draws. Bunch of pencils in his fist. Drawings scattered around him.*

FRANK *enters, in pyjamas, hiding something behind his back. Silence.*

FRANK. Uncle George caught a turbot. On the way in. We were uptiding over the sand bar. Got a nice box of mackerel. Few lobsters. Half a sack of scallops for that posh new restaurant on the front. All of a sudden he says, 'Eh Frank, let her drift a while. Got this feeling', he says. Ten minutes later there she is, big as a shield. Mouth like a steel trap. ''Tis a miracle', says George. 'Grab the bugger', I says. Turbot's a money fish.

Beat.

They all laughed. 'What you got there, George, a turbot?' 'Thass right', he says, 'lovely turbot from the Lord'. Peter Ford walks over. 'Look out', he says, 'George's only gone and got hisself another turbot from the Lord'. I says, 'You leave him be, Peter.' He says, 'Frank, you didn't buy him that on the quay, did you? Thass hardly fishing, is it Frank?' I says, 'I'll tell you whass hardly fishing, boy, 'tis your fancy sonars, and scanners going blip, and floppy fucking discs on the floor, thass hardly fishing in my book.' George stands there. Big stupid grin. Bloody great turbot under one arm, dripping on the juke-box.

He sings a bit of Dolly Parton.

'Here you come again – looking better than a body has a right to . . .'

Beat.

Anyway 'tis in the bath if you want a look. Your mother says she's allergic.

Pause.

You'll pore your eyes out, boy.

BILLY (*nods*). Mmm.

FRANK *brings out ship in a bottle from behind his back. Lays it in front of* BILLY.

FRANK. 'Tis a ship. In a bottle.

BILLY *picks it up. Hesitates. Offers it back to* FRANK.

No – no, 'tis for you. Juss finished her in the cellar. Kept it a secret. I made it for you.

BILLY *offers* FRANK *a drawing.*

No, I don't want that. You keep that in here. Look –

FRANK *takes bottle.*

FRANK. This is for you. A present. Put the picture down. I did this. 'Tis meant to be – put your pencils down –

BILLY (*nods*). Mmm –

FRANK. Put 'em down, then –

BILLY (*nods*). Mmm –

FRANK. 'Tis meant to be a model of the –

FRANK *snatches* BILLY*'s pencils, slams them on the floor.*

The rigging is the difficult bit. See? 'Tis fiddly. It can drive you up the wall, doing that –

FRANK *puts the bottle in* BILLY*'s hands.*

'Tis the ship Lord Nelson won the war with. 'The Victory'. I – made something, boy – for you. You understand?

BILLY (*nods*). Mmm.

Beat.

FRANK. So what do you think, then?

BILLY *turns the bottle in his hands.*

What do you think?

Silence.

FRANK. What if we woke up dead? You wanna be put away? That what you want? I keep thinking – what have we done wrong? You tell me. This a reward, is it?

Beat.

Whass the use? You're lost. I'm alone, aren't I? Might as well be locked in a fridge.

Beat.

I want you here.

BILLY (*nods*). Mmm.

FRANK. Your mother says you belong in that school. Best place for you, she says.

BILLY *probes in bottle with pencil.*

I says to her, 'What are we, dead?' She says whass the point if she can't even tell when you're unhappy. Your own mother, for Chrissake, shouldn't your own mother know if you're unhappy? Aren't I always in here saying 'For Chrissake, pull yourself together – '?

BILLY (*nods*). Mmm –

FRANK. When are you going to make an effort? She hits me across the face. 'You don't care', she says. I says, 'I care. I care about where the money's coming from for all this.' She says, 'Sell that boat.'

Pause.

I says, 'I aren't dead, am I?'

Pause. BILLY *is trying to get the ship out with a pencil.*

What are you doing? What are you doing that for? No, don't, don't do that, keep it in – don't pull that – keep it in the, no, keep it in the – oh for fu –

BILLY'*s pulling bits of ship out.*

Look, 'tis a ship in a bottle, see? 'Tis the bleeding 'Victory' in a bottle, thass the point, 'tis inside the – and the point is, 'tis really difficult, 'tis like magic, and you're meant to say, 'Eh dad, how the fuck did you – ?' Forget it. You've broken it.

Abruptly FRANK *grabs handful of pencils, breaks them in two, throws pieces in* BILLY'*s face.* BILLY *clutches bottle, rocking gently. He offers a drawing to* FRANK.

Get off.

BILLY *rocks. Silence.*

BILLY. Nn – nng – ng –

FRANK. Why won't you be my son?

BILLY. Gg – gg – gi – giff –

FRANK. Give.

BILLY. Giff –

FRANK. Give.

BILLY. Give –

FRANK. What?

With a great effort BILLY *blurts it out.*

BILLY. Give her back.

FRANK *stares.* BILLY *rocks.*

THREE

white horses

Cliff-top garden along the coast. Day. Lawn-mower on the grass. Box full of peas in pods, colander on top. We are listening to ANNIE's *voice, reading 'Distant Howling', a poem by Miroslav Holub.*

ANNIE'S VOICE: In Alsace,
   on 6th July 1885,
   a rabid dog knocked down
   the nine-year-old Joseph Meister
   and bit him fourteen times.
   Meister was the first patient
   saved by Pasteur
   with his vaccine, in thirteen
   progressive doses
   of the attenuated virus . . .

ANNIE *enters with can of petrol. Fills lawn-mower fuel tank, hands trembling. Her voice continues.*

Pasteur died of ictus
ten years later.
The janitor Meister
fifty-five years later
committed suicide
when the Germans occupied
his Pasteur Institute
with all those poor dogs.
Only the virus
remained above it all.

ANNIE's *hands are shaking, slopping petrol. She drops the can.*

ANNIE. Please . . .

She takes out cigarettes. KATHLEEN *enters.*

KATHLEEN. Soup's nearly ready. She says 'tis going on the table in four / minutes,

ANNIE. Okay –

KATHLEEN. like it or not, / she says.

ANNIE. I'm almost finished.

KATHLEEN. Looks great.

KATHLEEN *sets petrol-can upright.*

Got it all over the grass here. Thass not very clever, / is it?

ANNIE. No. Sorry.

ANNIE *fumbling with lighter.*

KATHLEEN. I wish you wouldn't smoke –

ANNIE. I'm not, I just need a cigarette now and then, okay? Don't look at me like that –

KATHLEEN. Like what?

KATHLEEN *takes lighter.*

Come away from the petrol, stupid.

KATHLEEN *lights* ANNIE's *cigarette.*

You're trembling –

ANNIE. Am I – ?

KATHLEEN. Look at your hand.

ANNIE *touches* KATHLEEN's *hair.*

Why don't you give up?

ANNIE. I suppose I / should –

KATHLEEN. 'Tis really pathetic.

ANNIE. I like them.

ANNIE *smokes.* KATHLEEN *looks out to sea.*

KATHLEEN. White horses, look.

Pause.

I saw you crying this morning. I went past your room, the door was open. You had your head against the wall.

Beat.

Tide's turning. Should be some surf.

ANNIE. You're not going swimming?

KATHLEEN. Might do. If I can get past the muck.

Beat.

I can't stand to see you cry.

ANNIE. Have you touched your homework this summer?

KATHLEEN. Yeah.

ANNIE. Have you?

KATHLEEN. Yes, sort of. I've still got that history project –

ANNIE. What about?

KATHLEEN. I dunno. History I should think.

ANNIE. Have you started?

KATHLEEN. I've been thinking.

ANNIE. So you haven't / started –

KATHLEEN. I've done all the thinking. God.

ANNIE. I might have an idea.

KATHLEEN. It has to be my / own idea.

ANNIE. You know my collection of old glass bottles – ?

KATHLEEN. The stuff in the attic?

ANNIE. Yes –

KATHLEEN. I'm not clearing out the attic.

ANNIE. Okay.

Pause.

KATHLEEN. Are they worth anything?

Beat.

Tch. I'll think about it, okay?

ANNIE *fetches box of peas.*

Why don't you come and eat? I've made carrot and orange for us. Gran wanted oxtail, I said well we bloody don't. She's gone and done a whole tin for herself. If it goes cold she'll / blame me –

ANNIE *kneels, scoops out pile of pea-pods, starts shelling.*

ANNIE. It'll be nicer cold. I / prefer it.

KATHLEEN. She'll be wild.

Beat.

ANNIE. When a child recovers from chicken pox, what happens is the virus remains dormant inside a collection of nerves in the spine. And then years later – for some reason – it comes alive again. But worse. Because shingles is far worse. You can get a really painful rash across here –

Runs her hand over her stomach.

ANNIE. 'A Belt of Roses from Hell'.

KATHLEEN *kneels.*

KATHLEEN. Mum, I don't want to be a doctor.

ANNIE. You know I went abroad to work for a while –

KATHLEEN. Yeah, India –

ANNIE. Pakistan.

KATHLEEN. Same difference.

ANNIE. Long before you, of course. Before your father –

KATHLEEN. Miserable sod.

ANNIE *scoops out pile of pea-pods for* KATHLEEN. *She picks up a pea-pod. Starts shelling. Pause.*

ANNIE. When I first went out there, they'd developed this problem with our milk powder. You see, we'd carefully weaned them from the culture of breast-feeding, and flogged them wholesale The Culture of Infant Formula. This is us. Japan. Holland. Massive campaigns. Everywhere you looked, huge posters of white naked babies hugging tins. So simple, so cheap. Just add water.

Beat.

In the villages nearly all the water is badly polluted. They can't read the instructions on the tins. They can't afford to waste kerosene boiling water. The feeding bottles aren't sterile. The Formula gets mixed all wrong with contaminated water. Suddenly there are all these babies – thousands and thousands – with chronic diarrhoea.

Beat.

Maybe we should have improved the water supply. In the event what we did was drastically improve the supply of drugs. It was a heaven-sent opportunity. We steeped the whole country in our latest anti-diarrhoea solutions.

Beat.

You've got a maggot.

KATHLEEN *rolls maggot between finger and thumb. Flicks it away.* ANNIE *continues shelling.*

The mothers didn't come to us. In Karachi you don't go to the hospital if you're ill, you go to the shoe-mender's. You buy your medicine over the cobbler's counter. Nobody bothers with prescriptions. The trouble was, some of the stuff they got hold of . . . Oh the companies advertised it, they said it would work, and it does – in adults. It was a drug which freezes intestinal function. It's not meant for babies at all.

Beat.

By the time the mothers did come to us it was always too late. So each day I worked there, six hundred babies were dying from exactly the same condition. And it was us.

Beat.

You're not doing very well. Shall I take some of yours – ?

ANNIE *takes handful of pea-pods from* KATHLEEN*'s pile.* KATHLEEN *slaps them from* ANNIE*'s hand.*

KATHLEEN. What am I supposed to do?

ANNIE *picks up pea-pods in silence.*

ANNIE. They have a way of staring. It may be only three hours, two hours before they die. Their eyes look straight into / yours,

KATHLEEN. Stop it –

ANNIE. they are wide open and they are perfectly still. It's like something has taken hold of your heart, squeezing it tighter and / tighter and

KATHLEEN. Stop it, will you – ?

ANNIE. you are falling off a cliff and they are staring into your eyes but you are falling and they are saying I didn't ask for this I didn't ask to be born and you are saying . . . you are saying . . . what are we doing?

MARIA *enters. One leg bandaged. Jabbing at the garden with her walking stick.*

MARIA. Something's been eating my spinach.

Beat.

Why is this grass going in straight lines? It's neurotic.

Pause.

Well I can't stand here all day gossiping. 'Sesame Street' is on.

She picks up colander.

I told you we were too late. These were ready at least a fortnight ago. Look at the size of them. What do you propose we do? Spit them at each other, perhaps, with our pea-shooters?

She starts to go.

Oh I'm afraid lunch is over. I have eaten my oxtail soup all up. It was delicious and so hot. I burned my mouth.

She goes off.

KATHLEEN. Christ. I'll go after her, shall I? Give her lemon bon-bon, or something.

KATHLEEN *stands to go.*

ANNIE. Do you ever think there are monsters, Kathy?

KATHLEEN. What?

ANNIE. Sometimes I think there are monsters.

Beat.

KATHLEEN. I don't know what you want me to say.

She starts to go.

ANNIE. Kathy – ?

ANNIE *goes to* KATHLEEN. *Holds her.* KATHLEEN *cannot return it, embarrassed and uncomfortable.*

KATHLEEN. Hey. Hey, stop. Come on, don't. Don't. Hey –

KATHLEEN *trying to release herself.*

For God's sake. You're crushing me –

She pushes ANNIE *away.*

ANNIE. I'm fine. I'm fine –

KATHLEEN. For God's sake –

KATHLEEN *runs off.* ANNIE *stares out to sea.*

FOUR

painting by numbers

ANNIE *dreams. Bavarian landscape. She stands on a street, black bag in hand. A sick child there, shivering in a blanket. Also* HITLER *before an easel, painting. A small table near him, bottle of wine, picnic hamper, plate of sandwiches.*

HITLER (*making mistake*). Blast –

> *Notices* ANNIE.

Where have you been? We've been waiting hours.

> *Goes to sick child.*

Come here. Come along, come along, I won't bite.

> ANNIE *approaches.*

What would you call that? I want an expert opinion.

> ANNIE *tends sick child.* HITLER *fetches plate of sandwiches. Takes a bite of one.*

Would you like a cucumber sandwich? No, quite right. The English contribution to civilization. Water and wind. So. What do you think?

ANNIE. 'Herpes varicella'.

HITLER. Ooer –

ANNIE. Chicken pox.

HITLER. I beg your pardon?

ANNIE. Chicken pox.

HITLER. Chicken pox?

> *Beat.*

Not the plague, then? I thought by the look of him it had to be the plague. Or at the very least, syphilis –

ANNIE (*to child*). Nothing to worry / about –

HITLER. Look, are you sure – ?

ANNIE. It always looks much worse than it is. Have you had it?

HITLER. Are you trying to be funny?

ANNIE. He's a little feverish. Tell his mother – bicarb in a cool bath. And dab the spots with calamine lotion if he scratches, / he'll

HITLER. Me?

ANNIE. be fine in a few days.

> *Beat.*

HITLER. Is that it?

ANNIE. Yes.

HITLER. Well I could've done that. Should have been a doctor.

He goes to table, pours two glasses of wine.

Would you care to join me?

Offers glass to ANNIE. *She takes it.*

Tell me. Do you know the theory of the syphilitic tendency?

ANNIE. Yes, / I've read –

HITLER. Fascinating –

ANNIE. Yes –

HITLER. Absolutely fascinating.

Beat.

I got it off Hess. The theory.

He chinks her glass and drinks.

Hess informs me – he's off being rubbed in aromatic oils, some Scandinavian half-wit plunging his greasy fingers into his arse, not my cup of tea at all – however, Hess says the whole thing turns on a disturbing question. Is it reasonable to assume that no-one, no-one in your family ancestry ever contracted syphilis?

Beat.

Makes you think, doesn't it?

ANNIE. Yes.

HITLER. The family heirloom. The signature of an almost forgotten age. A nice bit of tat from the master bedroom, as it were. And suddenly there you are, beginning to manifest deeply rooted symptoms. Tendencies. Tics. Itches. Small habits revealing to the world your shamelessly peccant pedigree. Your knee shivers uncontrollably under the dinner table. Doesn't it? Or your teeth feel sticky and you begin to think there's a slug inside a cavity.

He mops his brow.

Isn't it hot?

ANNIE *nods.*

What is the correct response to such a theory, I wonder? Hmmn?

ANNIE. I don't / know.

HITLER. For every rule of history there must be one honourable and glorious exception. Us. You and I – we do not itch, do we? No clandestine scratchings under the bedclothes. There are no slugs in our mouths.

Beat.

The people around us, however. Our neighbours, perhaps. They
could be carriers. Do you know what I mean? That poor child.
At this very moment, something could be clawing its way to the
surface. Cubism.

ANNIE. I'm sorry – ?

HITLER. Bolshevik art. Nature observed from the Parisian gutter.
The French transmit their syphilis to the canvas. And through
the canvas to their entire culture. I, on the other hand, I am
painting God. Look around you. This landscape. This country.
So beautiful – and yet – so much work to be done.

Pause. He contemplates his painting. Rumble of thunder.

Oh but look. Look at it, look at this feeble shit. Where are the
storms? Where are the heavens running with rivers of blood?
Where's the opera? Pathetic, watery whimsy – Christ, I'm
worse than Claude Monet. I must have life –

Beat.

Wait a minute. You. Yes. Why not – ?

He takes ANNIE *by the arm. Positions her next to sick child.*

You don't mind, do you? Helping me? Just stand here –

Gives her the black bag.

And this of course. Now look at me. Shoulders back. Bit more.
Pride. That's it, good. Good –

Returning to easel.

HITLER. Now don't move. Absolutely still. Whatever you do,
don't smile. Pride. Pride and ice –

He paints.

Yes. Yes. Perfect. The doctor with her black bag, comforting
the worker's poor sick son. And behind you, in the distance,
almost concealed in a dark wood – I'll have a hospital. Yes.
A railway line – and a hospital. We'll treat them all. All the
children of darkness. And through the window of a cottage,
here – you can just see a man. The scholar sitting in his study.
It is me. I'll call it – 'The Will in Nature' . . .

He paints.

Together my dear, you and I, we'll arouse the people's will to
become perfect. Once will is gone, all is gone. Life is war.

Closer rumble of thunder. It starts to rain on HITLER. *He
makes a mistake.*

Blast –

Makes another mistake.

Blast –

Rains harder. Makes another mistake.

Oh fuck it –

ANNIE *is crying silently.*

HITLER. That was you. You moved. What are you crying for?

ANNIE *goes and picks up petrol can. Lightning. Thunder clap.*

It's only a shower.

HITLER *goes.* ANNIE *seemingly back in the cliff-top garden. Standing beside lawn-mower and can of petrol, black bag with her.* ANNIE *pours petrol over black bag.*

FIVE

slugs

A fisherman, GEORGE LUCKETT, *alone. He sings part of the Methodist hymn, 'Let the Lower Lights'. Alternatively, a small group of congregationers, in church, singing in harmony.*

GEORGE. Brightly beams our Father's mercy
  From His lighthouse evermore;
  But to us He gives the keeping
  Of the lights along the shore.

  Let the lower lights be burning,
  Send a gleam across the wave;
  Some poor fainting, struggling seaman
  You may rescue, you may save.

  Dark the night of sin has settled,
  Loud the angry billows roar;
  Eager eyes are watching, longing,
  For the lights along the shore.

  Let the lower lights be burning,
  Send a gleam across the wave;
  Some poor fainting, struggling seaman
  You may rescue, you may save.

GEORGE *goes.*

Cliff-top garden. A patch of scorched grass and ash where
ANNIE *was left.* KATHLEEN *there, unkempt and dirty, no*
shoes. Wearing some of ANNIE's *clothes. One of* ANNIE's
necklaces. She examines contents of small wooden box.

FRANK *and* GEORGE *enter.* GEORGE *carries string of*
mackerel. They wait in silence. Finally.

FRANK. Fish.

They wait.

GEORGE. Fish.

They wait.

FRANK. 'Tis Mister Luckett, look –

GEORGE. With the fish.

FRANK (*to* KATHLEEN). Where's – uh – where's the old woman
    to?

GEORGE. Mrs Schweniger, you old crone – !

GEORGE *goes to look at patch of scorched grass.*

This where she – ?

Beat.

We – uh – we had a woman, didn't we Frank?

FRANK. Eh?

GEORGE. We had that woman.

FRANK. Woman – ?

GEORGE. Drove her car straight into the harbour, didn't she?

FRANK. Right.

GEORGE. Right.

FRANK. By mistake –

GEORGE. By mistake, but – she drowned. She drowned.

FRANK. Couldn't get her out the mud, see.

GEORGE. You dived in, Frank.

FRANK. I dived in.

GEORGE. She was only an emmet.

Beat.

'Twas an orange M.G.B.

GEORGE *chuckles.*

FRANK. Nobody found that funny for ages.

Beat.

GEORGE. She's with God now, I expect.

FRANK. Look we brought the old woman's fish. Where's she to, eh? 'Cus them mackerel, they're about ready to walk back in the sea on their own accord –

GEORGE. Mother's got me a steak and kidney pudding sitting on the table, Frank –

FRANK. Tedn' nature –

GEORGE *tosses fish onto ground.*

GEORGE. Tedn' nature, is it Frank? Not on a Friday.

BILLY *enters, humming Cornish folk tune. He sits to draw.* GEORGE *joins in with* BILLY*'s tune. Finally adds words.*

GEORGE. ' . . . your youthful days – '

FRANK. 'Tis their favourite song –

GEORGE *sings.*

GEORGE. 'Oh come all you young men,
With your wicked ways,
And sow all your wild oats
In your youthful days – '

'Tis Bright Millar's song, idn' it, Billy?

BILLY (*nods*). Mmm –

GEORGE (*to* KATHLEEN). You know the story of Bright Millar? Tell her, Frank –

FRANK *shakes head at* GEORGE.

Our dad told us. And he was forever telling it to some silly emmet sat in 'The Farmer's / Arms' –

KATHLEEN. I was born here.

GEORGE. You hear that, Frank? She was born here and she don't even know the story of Bright Millar. Tell her, / Frank –

FRANK. Not now, George. Mrs Schweniger – !

GEORGE. He lived round here. Coupla hundred year ago. There's an old rock in a wall down Trevone, got his name on. His tears left it / there.

FRANK. George –

GEORGE. He was a sailor boy, weren't he Billy?

BILLY (*nods*). Mmm –

BILLY *draws the story.*

GEORGE. He came home from war with some madness germ
    inside. So they shut him in the asylum. That old place they had
    once, over St. Nun's Pool. Every Sunday there was a
    performance. A kind of circus. They'd bring out all the lunatics.
    One was given a whip and he made the others dance and do
    back-flips while Bright sang his song. People came from all
    over. Far as London. They paid a penny to watch. But Bright
    runs away, don't he Billy?

BILLY (*nods*). Mmm –

GEORGE. He runs back here, and 'tis here they catch him. He has
    a fit, he's shaking, he's dying / see –

FRANK. For God's sake, / George –

GEORGE. They all see the Devil in the boy's plague. But when
    he's dead they tie him to a post and put him out there on the
    headland –

GEORGE *points out to sea.*

GEORGE. 'Stepper Point'.

Unnoticed, MARIA *enters.*

People round here believe the touch of a dead boy's hand is
    virtue. So the town fetch out every sick man and woman.
    There's a line of 'em from the head to the harbour. And while
    the children dance round the post, Bright's hand is curing every
    illness in the town.

GEORGE *ruffles* BILLY*'s hair.*

True story, idn' it Frank? True as he's sitting here. Suffer the /
    little children –

FRANK. Shut up, George –

GEORGE. Dad woulda told it better, eh Frank? Dad could weave a
    tale round your throat and pull it till you thought you were
    going to / choke.

FRANK. Mrs Schweni – !

Sees MARIA *there.*

MARIA. You fish men do not tire making up such stories?

Beat.

FRANK. Folklore's the only industry we got left. Idn' it?

MARIA *sprinkles little piles of salt on the ground.*

MARIA. And now this shouting in my garden –

FRANK. I rang / the doorbell –

MARIA. You think you are both so important to shout in my / garden?

FRANK. I rang the doorbell, / Mrs Schweniger –

MARIA. But I am not in the house, / I am

FRANK. I realize th –

MARIA. down the garden.

She sprinkles salt.

FRANK. We got other people to see too, you know. You're not the only old woman in Cornwall eats our fish –

MARIA. I'm sure this / is true –

FRANK. You name me one other fisherman in Padstow daft enough to walk mackerel all the way up here, / same as us.

MARIA. But you haven't been for weeks.

FRANK. No. No, well I didn't think you'd want . . . not in the circumstances –

GEORGE. Anyway 'tis the boat.

MARIA. What about it?

FRANK. Nothing. I got a bit of trouble, thass all – with the / bank.

GEORGE. Stella keeps on to him, sell the / boat.

FRANK. Sell it? I'm still trying to buy the / fucking thing –

GEORGE. And there's the men in Padstow, / working

FRANK. No there aren't –

GEORGE. with Satan. / They want to

FRANK. No they aren't, George –

GEORGE. stop us going / out.

FRANK. George –

GEORGE. They control everything, this one family. They think they own the fish. But we know whass behind it, don't we Frank?

FRANK. 'Tis like a cartel. I can't get in –

GEORGE. Tedn' right. He's in the Rotary Club –

FRANK. Right. I am. I should be allowed, shouldn't I? Aren't I in the bloody Rotary Club?

MARIA *looks up from sprinkling salt.*

MARIA. Is there a hole in your boat?

FRANK. Eh?

MARIA. You have sprung a leak?

FRANK. No –

MARIA. I'm quite happy to buy my fish from Mr Orchard, if you two cannot manage / my orders.

FRANK. Now wait a minute –

GEORGE (*with* FRANK). Mr Orchard wouldn't sell a tin of pilchards to a kraut on account of his father. With respect.

MARIA. Oh I like this phrase so much. 'With respect'. It is England, isn't it?

She returns to sprinkling salt.

GEORGE. His father was a bombardier, see. Lancasters. You muss remember Gregory Peck –

MARIA. You are obsessed with the war when you go to your other old women? Or only when you come / into my garden?

GEORGE. If you had to choose one man to drop a bomb to save your life, you'd choose Charlie Orchard's dad.

MARIA. We are being hostile today, aren't we?

Beat.

GEORGE. What are you doing?

MARIA. A slug, Mr Luckett, is a good for nothing.

GEORGE. Whass that stuff?

MARIA. Salt. See Kathleen? Watch the slugs dissolve.

GEORGE. Not a very Christian thing / to do –

MARIA. You hear them complaining?

FRANK. They're juss slugs, / George –

MARIA. Besides, I don't think God minds. The slug is superfluous. Überflüssig. Like your appendix, grumbling because it is sorry to be alive. Or your wisdom tooth, inflicting upon you the pointless agony of knowledge. If I were a slug, I would want someone to pour salt on me.

GEORGE. God forgives you.

MARIA. I must remember to thank Him.

KATHLEEN *is with* BILLY. *He is silently counting things on the horizon.*

There. Now they are water again. Human beings are seventy-five per cent water. Sometimes it is wise to bear this in mind when one of them is talking to you.

MARIA *flicks remains of slug away with stick.*

GEORGE. I've had all my wisdom teeth out.

Beat.

FRANK. Time to go home, George. You go on home, now. I'll juss get paid.

GEORGE. All right, Frank. God loves you. God loves everyone. Even the krauts.

GEORGE *goes off.*

KATHLEEN. Whass he doing?

FRANK *looks at* BILLY.

FRANK. Counting.

KATHLEEN. Whass he counting? What are you counting?

FRANK. 'Tis anything he sees more than one of. Is it the trees, Billy? Or the rooks? 'Tis the rooks I / reckon –

KATHLEEN. People with syphilis can't stop counting things.

FRANK. Eh?

KATHLEEN. Mum said.

MARIA *starts to go off.*

FRANK. Eh, where you going? Where's my money to? You owe three / months –

MARIA. But my fish are lying in the dirt, Mr Luckett. I'm going to turn the compost, Kathleen.

MARIA *goes off.*

FRANK. What about my money?

Pause.

Come on, Billy. You coming? You wanna stay here a bit – ?

KATHLEEN. He's all right.

FRANK. Suit yourselves.

Beat.

You're going to cure him, are you?

KATHLEEN. Might do.

Beat. FRANK *starts to go. Hesitates by patch of scorched grass.*

She was – she was beautiful, your mother. I coulda got her in the Rotary Club. No-one wants a kraut, but – I woulda put a word in. 'Course, people round here, they really know how to bear a grudge. German, French, Spanish. 'Tis all the same. 'Tis all one lousy memory, idn' it?

Beat.

And the fact everyone's a cunt.

FRANK *goes off.* BILLY*'s anxiety rising.*

KATHLEEN. 'Tis okay –

Picks up BILLY*'s sketch-pad.*

KATHLEEN. 'Tis good, what is it? House? Whose house? Your house – ?

BILLY *shakes his head.*

KATHLEEN. Not a house. Castle? A castle – ?

BILLY *shakes his head.*

Who's this? Face at the window. That you – ?

BILLY *shakes his head.*

KATHLEEN. Me?

BILLY. Nnn –

KATHLEEN. You. You're in the house – ?

BILLY *shakes his head.*

BILLY. Nnn –

KATHLEEN. The castle –

BILLY. Mmmb – b –

KATHLEEN. What? Tell me. Is it you? Is it a prison – ?

BILLY *hums* BRIGHT*'s song.*

KATHLEEN. Bright – ?

BILLY *nods.*

Bright. Bright's house –

BILLY *nods.*

KATHLEEN. St. Nun's Pool.

Beat. She lays drawing down.

'Tis creepy.

Pause.

My mum set fire to herself.

Suddenly dances wildly.

Draw me –

As she dances.

I saw two boys once. Throwing a black ball of rags up and down the slide –

BILLY *picks up* KATHLEEN's *wooden box. Removes glass bottle.*

They were kicking the ball on the ground. Go on, draw me –

She dances.

But 'twasn't a ball, was it? 'Twas a kitten.

She stops dancing. BILLY *twisting and squeezing glass bottle.*

Careful. 'Tis valuable. I got lots.

BILLY. Vvv – Vv – 'Vic . . . tree' –

KATHLEEN *tries to rescue bottle.*

KATHLEEN. You'll break it. Let go. Let go, 'tis mine. 'Tis mine, fucking hell –

Snatches bottle away.

KATHLEEN. You fucking syphilis – !

BILLY *runs off.*

Billy – ? Billy . . . ?

Pause. KATHLEEN *lies back on the grass.*

SIX

a fiend hid in a cloud

KATHLEEN *dreams. She is inside St. Nun's Pool Asylum. A great house of confinement, beginning of the nineteenth century. Distant cries and whispers. Sudden distant screams and laughter. Sound of boy singing* BRIGHT's *song brokenly.*

A couple shuffle through, supporting one another.

> BRIGHT MILLAR *is there. Filthy, feverish, nothing on his feet. State of syphilitic delirium, rubbing himself.*

BRIGHT. Get 'em – get 'em off – get 'em off me – !

> KATHLEEN *makes a move towards him.*

Stay there! Don't come near. They'll get you. Get in your eyes. They live in the walls. The ground. See 'em? Don't! Mustn't touch. Fingers mustn't touch –

KATHLEEN. Mum – !

BRIGHT. Don't need you – !

KATHLEEN. Where are / you, mum – !

BRIGHT. I'm a good boy. I can heal / myself,

KATHLEEN. Help him – !

BRIGHT. got medicine –

> BRIGHT *takes out phial.*

Get it from a dog. Harry showed me. Makes you walk on air. Over the snakes –

KATHLEEN. Snakes – ?

BRIGHT. Milk of dog. Dog's milk –

> *Drinks medicine. Thrusts hands under armpits, rocking.*

KATHLEEN. Whass wrong – ?

BRIGHT. Good boy. Lucky boy. He's got demons in his blood. You want some? You can have some of mine. I got plenty –

> BRIGHT *rocking, shuddering. Abruptly scampers and snatches up mackerel left by* GEORGE.

KATHLEEN. Thass our fish –

BRIGHT. Finders keepers –

> *Eats greedily.*

KATHLEEN. No more snakes – ?

BRIGHT. Come and go, don't they? Gone back in now.

KATHLEEN. I'm not scared. I'm making this all up. You're in my garden –

BRIGHT. Garden – ?

> *Giggles.*

This is my garden. You're in my garden now. They put you in the madhouse, girl. They don't put juss anyone in here, you know. Have to be special, see –

KATHLEEN. I'm looking for my mother.

BRIGHT. She's an orphan. Orphan Annie. There's one of you in here only pissed in a pulpit. Been here ten years. Pricey piss, I call it. They chuck you away, don't they? I seen it in Plymouth. Poor tossers leaving their kids on shop-corner doorsteps. Babes in boxes. Always on a Sunday. So God comes down. Picks you up. Drops you in here. Wipes His hands on His jodhpurs. Fucks off. Never get to heaven in a grocer's box –

BRIGHT *suddenly rigid.*

KATHLEEN. What is it – ?

Pulls KATHLEEN *down beside him. Wait. The couple return, shuffling through, supporting one another.*

BRIGHT. They're no-one. They're in love.

Moment of embarrassment. BRIGHT *pulls away.*

I touched your arm.

Beat.

Keep away from Chyle. She'll take you –

KATHLEEN. Why?

BRIGHT. Experiments. We're all Chyle's children, down here –

Begins to touch himself distractedly.

I listen to 'em at night. You hear 'em scream. 'Tis so far down. A scream gets stuck in the walls. They say she sucks it out of you –

Rubbing himself.

Out of here –

Touches top of head.

Sucks it out of here –

KATHLEEN *holds him. touches him. Caresses. Holds his hand where he rubs himself. He moans softly, rocking.*

KATHLEEN. Don't . . . don't . . . you'll make it worse . . . no . . . no, let me . . . let me . . . let me –

KATHLEEN *embracing* BRIGHT, *wanting to go further. Suddenly interrupted by noise from above.* BRIGHT *about to scream.* KATHLEEN *puts hand over his mouth.* CHYLE's voice.

CHYLE (*off*). Bright? Don't hide from me, it's so childish –

KATHLEEN (*whispers*). Chyle – ?

> BRIGHT *nods.*

CHYLE (*off*). I've something for you, Bright. Some fish –

> CHYLE *moving away.*

> How can I be expected to keep trace of my experiments amongst all these cretins – !

> *Pause.* KATHLEEN *takes hand away.*

KATHLEEN. Shit –

> KATHLEEN *on top of* BRIGHT, *looking into his eyes, expectant moment.*

BRIGHT. She can't be a real doctor, can she? She's only a woman. 'Tis against the rules. (*Shouts up.*) You're not real! You're not a man! I coulda been a doctor –

KATHLEEN. Tedn' that easy –

BRIGHT. Tedn' hard to be a cunt, is it?

> *Beat.*

KATHLEEN. When I was seven I said if my mum's a doctor, I'm going to live for ever.

BRIGHT. How old are you?

KATHLEEN. Dunno. Nearly fifteen.

BRIGHT. I'm fourteen. Been in here two years. I think 'tis my birthday –

> KATHLEEN *kisses him. Starts touching him again.* BRIGHT *talks as* KATHLEEN *explores his body, both increasingly turned on.*

> My dad was a cunt. He sent me away on a ship. Thass how I met Harry. I was only eleven –

KATHLEEN. Harry – ?

BRIGHT. Harry Nelson. I was his boy. I was at Trafalgar, me. I took care of him, all the way to England. Had to stop the sun burning him up, see. We used all the rum. Got home and his body was –

> *Beat.*

> I kept his face covered. I could feel him staring up at me. It was me he kissed. When he was dying. He loved me. He loved me –

KATHLEEN *kisses him.*

I'm going to run away. You going to run away – ?

The KEEPER *is there.* BRIGHT *pushes* KATHLEEN *off him.*

Oh fuck. The keeper –

KEEPER *advances, brandishing stick.*

KEEPER. Got you, you dirty little bastard –

KEEPER *beats* BRIGHT *with stick.*

KATHLEEN. No – !

BRIGHT *crying out.*

No! Leave him, you're hurting him – ! 'Twas me, 'twas me – !

KEEPER *drags* BRIGHT *away.*

Stop hurting him, 'twas me . . . leave us alone, stop hurting . . . stop hurting . . .

KATHLEEN *coming out of dream.* MARIA *is there. She holds* KATHLEEN.

MARIA. I know, I know it hurts, I know you hurt, it is good now. It is good. You have a good cry now. A good cry. This is very good for you now –

KATHLEEN. There was a boy . . . in the garden –

MARIA. He is gone / now –

KATHLEEN. He wasn't in the garden –

MARIA. Oh –

KATHLEEN. He's in that horrible place –

MARIA. Not a garden / at all -

KATHLEEN. He's sick –

MARIA. Oh dear –

KATHLEEN. There's some kind of doctor –

MARIA. Good –

KATHLEEN. They beat him – !

KATHLEEN *pounds at* MARIA *with fists.*

Beat him and beat him and beat – !

MARIA *trying to stop her hands.*

MARIA. All right, dear, all right – it is over. It is all over now –

KATHLEEN *rips off necklace, throws it at* MARIA.

KATHLEEN. Bright needs me – !

MARIA. Ah. Bright. Of course –

MARIA picks up necklace.

We have such bad dreams, the pair / of us.

KATHLEEN. He's in danger –

MARIA. But some things are just pictures, aren't they?

Beat.

I gave this to your mother. On the day she was married.

Beat. Offers it to KATHLEEN.

I think you want it back.

Presses necklace into KATHLEEN's hand. Notices half-eaten mackerel. KATHLEEN fetches wooden box, puts necklace inside. Stands on cliff-edge, staring out to sea.

Tch, look at that. Did somebody eat our fish?

KATHLEEN. He ate them –

MARIA. Not Mr Luckett? Poor man –

MARIA picks up fish.

I was going to make that funny fish pie. We have to keep the devil out of Cornwall. Ah well.

MARIA produces some wild mushrooms.

We'll make do with scrambled eggs on toast. But with wild mushrooms on top, look –

She goes to KATHLEEN. Pause.

I like to look at the sea after a storm. It is like a baby left alone to cry itself to sleep.

Beat. Produces sprig of mistletoe.

Mistletoe. What on earth is it doing here? It must be good luck. We'll hang it over our doors tonight so we have no more nightmares. They say a little bit on your pillow and you can see your future husband in a vision –

MARIA puts arm round KATHLEEN's shoulder. KATHLEEN goes rigid. MARIA has to take her arm away. KATHLEEN starts to go off. MARIA follows.

I'm going to make a cup of tea with some of the leaves, to help my leg. And all the slugs are gone. It's a start, isn't it?

They go off.

SEVEN

the pity of strangers

Cliff-top garden. MARIA *stalking starlings. Suddenly launches attack with her walking stick.*

MARIA. Get out – ! Get out, get out – !

> *Her bad leg gives way. She staggers, falls. Sees starling on ground. Picks it up.* KATHLEEN *there watching.*

Little English bird. You didn't know I could knock you from the sky, Mr Gregory Peck. Now I should bite your head off, perhaps –

> KATHLEEN *picks up walking stick.*

They were stealing our raspberries –

> KATHLEEN *swings stick violently.*

Yes! Yes! Good – ! I wanted to punish them too. They think every bloody thing in the garden is theirs.

> KATHLEEN *stops. Drops stick.*

I saw a picture of myself, Kathleen, with hundreds of starlings lying at my feet.

Offers starling.

It is only wounded. I can feel its heart. Would you like to make it better?

KATHLEEN. I'll put it on the television. Sit and watch what happens.

MARIA. All right, dear.

> KATHLEEN *goes off.* MARIA *struggling up as* FRANK *enters.* BILLY *trailing behind, clutching sketch-pad.* FRANK *carries package and bottle of clear spirit.*

Oh heavens. The return of the Luckett family. I assume you have come to drop a bomb on us – ?

> FRANK *gives* MARIA *walking stick.*

FRANK. Uh –

MARIA. Yes – ?

FRANK. About the other day –

MARIA. Yes – ?

FRANK. I, uh – look, I really wanted to say something –

MARIA. Yes – ?

FRANK. You know – how sorry I was.

Beat.

MARIA. I didn't give you your money –

FRANK. No, I didn't / come for –

MARIA. It must be a pony at / least –

FRANK. No. Look –

FRANK *offers package.*

Here. Take it –

MARIA. Why?

FRANK. 'Tis for you and the girl.

MARIA. Why?

FRANK. Well, because – you know –

Beat.

MARIA. This is your apology.

FRANK. Yeah –

MARIA. You behave insensitively –

FRANK. Yeah, right –

MARIA. In front of Kathleen –

FRANK. Sorry.

Beat.

MARIA. Where is your charming brother?

FRANK. Oh God. He's in church. He used to stand up and shout in the middle of the sermon. Maze as a brush. Now they let him give out the hymn books. Keep him quiet. Sorry.

MARIA. Hm. What would the English do with themselves if they could not spend the whole day apologizing?

FRANK. I dunno.

FRANK *holds out package.* MARIA *takes it, peers inside.*

Where's she to?

MARIA. Watching a bird on the television.

FRANK. Yeah, thass all he does.

MARIA. Half a salmon. Hm. You are only half sorry perhaps. I would have preferred the half with the head. Still. Never mind. I am gardening now, goodbye.

KATHLEEN *enters carrying small wooden box.*

KATHLEEN. 'Tis dead.

Shows BILLY *dead starling in box.*

She killed it.

KATHLEEN *kneels beside* BILLY. *Gives him starling to hold. Digs hole in flower-bed.*

FRANK. He likes her, look.

Beat.

I'll take him home –

MARIA. No, leave them. Where's the harm?

Pause.

FRANK. 'Tis three weeks now, idn' it? Three weeks?

MARIA. Four weeks.

Maria takes out tin of small cigars and lighter.

I am suffocating, aren't you?

She lights cigar.

FRANK. Yeah –

MARIA. This insufferable English air. It is like being hugged by a man you no longer love.

FRANK. Yeah. Yeah, 'tis close.

MARIA. So is this another apology for me?

FRANK. Eh? Oh, uh – no -

MARIA. Oh –

FRANK. No, I juss thought we – might have a drink / together –

MARIA. Ah. You are intending to seduce me.

FRANK. Uh – it hadn't occurred to / me, no –

MARIA. Why not?

FRANK. Uh – my wife distils it in the cellar.

FRANK *offers bottle.*

'Tis made from bananas and potatoes –

MARIA *sips.*

MARIA. Dreadful –

FRANK. It grows on you. Cherry blossom wine.

MARIA. Cherry – ?

FRANK. Secret ingredient. Shoe polish. She's a funny woman.

MARIA. The evil doings in the village cellars.

FRANK. We got gallons of it.

> FRANK *drinks.* KATHLEEN *and* BILLY *are burying starling. They cover grave with sandy ash from patch of scorched grass.*

MARIA. Would you be kind enough to put your salmon in the kitchen? You may run it under the tap and wrap it in newspaper –

> FRANK *nods, starts to go off with package.*

Oh and Mr Luckett – ? I have a wheelchair now. You'll find it in the sun-lounge. Would you bring it to me? My leg is hurting. My purse is on the draining board. Please take what you want.

> FRANK *goes off.*

MARIA. Now then. Would you two like to go down the garden? Take him to see the buzzard, Kathleen. Look for feathers together. I won't touch anything, I promise.

> KATHLEEN *goes off.* BILLY *follows, clutching sketch-pad.* MARIA *recalls verse from Bible.*

'Denn alles Fleisch es ist wie Gras und alle Herrlichkeit des Menschen wie des Grases Blumen. Das Gras ist verdorret und die Blume abgefallen.'

> *She is crying silently.* FRANK *enters pushing wheelchair.*

FRANK. You all right?

MARIA. All flesh is grass, Mr Luckett.

FRANK. Is it? Found these, look –

> FRANK *holds out two glasses.* MARIA *takes one.*

MARIA. Ice, too. How civilized –

FRANK. Nice glass –

> FRANK *fetches bottle.*

MARIA. Hm.

FRANK. Heavy.

> FRANK *pours.*

MARIA. My husband and I bought them in nineteen forty-six – just before we left. They are from Dresden. We managed to find one small corner shop, almost untouched.

They drink.

FRANK. My dad used to say he fought in three world wars against your lot. Stupid sod. I put the fish in the Daily Telegraph.

MARIA. I hope it is happy.

FRANK. I do the crossword.

MARIA. On your own? Put me in there, please.

FRANK *helps* MARIA *into wheelchair.*

I can't abide this contraption. My daughter insisted.

FRANK. That bandage wants a change –

MARIA. It's for support only.

FRANK. Whass wrong with it?

MARIA. It's going bad inside the bone marrow. Rotting – like compost. If I have a bad day I find a new bruise in the morning.

FRANK. 'Tis serious, then.

MARIA. It is called Myeloma. It is a nice word.

FRANK. Yeah, I suppose –

MARIA. To be precise, Mr Luckett, I have a Myelomatosis. It seems I am giving house room to a family of rogue plasma cells. Plasma cells are produced by the B lymphocytes in the bone marrow. They make antibodies which neutralize any foreign invader. They are the good guys in the war against infection. In Myeloma, however, the B lymphocytes decide to make, for no apparent reason, a great deal of unnecessary plasma –

FRANK. They think you got something, when you haven't –

MARIA. Exactly. My immune system has gone on the offensive. A swaggering army on a crusade, not knowing who to attack, no longer aware of what it is trying to save. There is massive over-production in the armament factory. The plasma cells are confused, so they are massing together in clumps inside my bone marrow, waiting for instructions. Tumours. They are grumbling, whispering behind their hands – 'What are we doing here?' 'I don't know, I thought you knew?' 'Me, how should I know?' They are uncomfortable, there is not enough room for them, so they are pushing out other cells, who wander about, homeless, until they wither and die. Meanwhile, the plasma cells, believing they must be there for a reason, are producing vast quantitites of their antibody. They are pouring it into my blood by the bucketful. My blood is awash with goodness. That is my disease. It is fascinating, no? My body has decided to defend itself against an enemy that doesn't exist.

FRANK. Sounds like you're enjoying it anyway –

MARIA. Oh I love those delicious television programmes, where they show the beating heart. And the hysterical nature programmes. All that fucking! Good health.

They drink.

FRANK. How long?

MARIA. Soon. I'm free to choose from a range of different infections. Pneumonia, probably.

FRANK. I'm sorry.

MARIA. Why? What have you done?

Beat.

FRANK. What about the girl?

MARIA. Kathleen and I barely know each other. I don't need the pity of a stranger.

FRANK. I mean what'll happen to her?

MARIA. She has an aunt in America. My youngest. I have sent for her. I am expecting her to take Kathleen away.

FRANK. Does she know that?

MARIA. Not yet. She has never met her aunt.

Beat.

FRANK. Well. Everyone wants to go to Disneyland.

Already building, sound of boys, off. Teasing and calling nastily. Shouts and laughter. KATHLEEN's voice shouting back. Something of the following discernible. Fast.

BOY 1 (*off*). Whass this – ?

KATHLEEN (*off*). Leave it –

BOY 2 (*off*). Give us it –

BOY 1 (*off*). Give us it, you –

KATHLEEN (*off*). Get off –

BOY 1 (*off*). Give us it, y'Nazi –

BOY 2 (*off*). She's crying –

BOY 1 (*off*). Y'cunt –

BOY 2 (*off*). Y'Nazi –

BOY 1 (*off*). Y'Nazi crying cunt –

BOY 2 (*off*). Y'Nazi crying kraut crunt –

BOY 1 (*off*). Crunt – ?

BOY 2 (*off*). Crunt – ?

BOY 1 (*off*). Y'crunt –

BOY 2 (*off*). Who you calling a crunt – ?

BOY 1 (*off*). You, y'crunt – !

    Boys laughing, off. KATHLEEN *runs in.*

KATHLEEN. Boys –

MARIA. What boys, what have / they done – ?

    BILLY *runs in, distressed. Sketch-book dishevelled, clutching two long buzzard feathers.*

KATHLEEN. Tore his picture up –

FRANK. They must have sneaked / along the cliff –

KATHLEEN. They called me a cunt –

MARIA (*to* FRANK). This word belongs to you, / I think –

FRANK. They're juss boys. / All right, Billy?

BILLY (*rocking*). Mmm –

KATHLEEN (*with* BILLY). They were horrible –

MARIA. Boys are horrible, Kathleen. Otherwise they wouldn't be / boys.

KATHLEEN. They pushed 'im / over –

FRANK. He's got to learn.

    FRANK *shouts off.*

    Out of it, you lot! Bugger off! Down the beach, go on! Go drown yourselves – !

    Laughter and jeering of boys, off, fading away.

FRANK. I expect they only wanted to play.

MARIA. She needs a friend, doesn't she – ?

KATHLEEN. I got a friend. Bright Millar. He's my friend.

    KATHLEEN *goes off.* BILLY *goes after her.*

MARIA. Bright Millar. Honestly, Mr Luckett. The things we tell our children.

    FRANK *fills glasses. They drink.*

FRANK. He – uh – he had a twin sister. She was – you know . . . still-born. I think he was sorta still-born too, except he kept on breathing. He juss – clung on for no reason. Silly sod.

Pause.

Her dad – he's buggered off, hasn't he – ?

MARIA. Oh yes – he has buggered off for some months now –

FRANK. He was a shit. If you don't mind me saying –

MARIA. No, I agree. He was a coward. But my daughter loved him. He is a coward. Her daughter hates him. So. There you are –

FRANK. The Treyarnons are a lousy family –

MARIA. Peter was all arms and cock. Quite ugly. Not like you at all.

FRANK. Eh?

MARIA *drains glass. Holds it out for more.* FRANK *pours.*

MARIA. So you have a good cock between your legs, Mr Luckett?

FRANK. You what – ?

MARIA. Or is it a big bad cock?

FRANK. A whopper.

MARIA. I think I'm getting a little pissed. Why not? Why should I give a bugger?

FRANK *stands over patch of scorched grass.*

I cannot say I loved my daughter.

FRANK. She looked after you, didn't she?

MARIA. I wouldn't let her near me. Little thin fingers, armed with a suppository.

FRANK. But she was good, wasn't she? Doctors have to be good –

MARIA. I'm afraid history isn't supporting you, Mr Luckett.

FRANK. Everybody down the surgery liked her. Billy liked / her –

MARIA. No. No, it isn't true, is it? She would come home crying.

FRANK. Why?

MARIA *drains her glass.*

MARIA. Push me.

FRANK. Eh – ?

MARIA. Push me, would you? I want to be nearer the edge –

FRANK *pushes,* MARIA *waves her stick.*

No quickly, take me round . . . faster, faster – !

FRANK. Keep your hair on –

MARIA. Oh you are hopeless! Come on, down there now, down there – !

FRANK *sweeps her quickly round garden, then down to cliff-edge. FRANK goes to fetch glasses, fills them again. Unnoticed, KATHLEEN and BILLY are back. They keep their distance.*

MARIA. Oh this isn't near enough. I can't see the rocks –

MARIA *climbs unsteadily out of wheelchair.* FRANK *returning with glasses.*

FRANK. You'll go over, you silly old goat –

MARIA *goes to edge. Poses.*

Come away / from there –

MARIA. What do you think?

FRANK. What the fuck are you doing?

MARIA. Tch, my breasts – they sag, no – ?

FRANK. Pardon – ?

MARIA. They are not firm. They are weak. They are / sagging –

FRANK. Look, you're too near the –

MARIA. Do they sag or not?

FRANK. They sag a bit!

MARIA. I'm afraid you'll never seduce me if you insist on being honest. Believe it or not, I used to be quite beautiful. This humiliating old rag once belonged to a film actress.

FRANK. You were never a film actress. Were you?

MARIA. During the war. I was in many films in the nineteen forties.

FRANK. Get away –

MARIA. I have hidden talents.

FRANK. You take your clothes off?

MARIA. You have to understand the kind of films they were making –

FRANK. War films.

MARIA. Patriotic films.

FRANK. Any good?

MARIA. Oh they were very popular. They said one of my films was seen by eighteen million people –

FRANK. Fuck me –

MARIA. That was in nineteen forty-one. I went to Hollywood after the war.

FRANK. She's been famous! Heidi Lamarr took her clothes off in nineteen thirty-three. She was the first –

MARIA. Ha! I knew it. Beneath all the mackerel lies a man of taste and discrimination –

FRANK. 'Ecstasy', weren't it – ?

MARIA. Wonderful film! I am talking to a buff –

FRANK. No, we used to have a calendar in the toilet.

> FRANK *drawn again to patch of scorched grass.* KATHLEEN *watching.* BILLY *has wooden box. Takes out glass bottle, fondles it.*

FRANK. So what did she make of it? Having such a famous mother?

MARIA. We never discussed it. Annie had no interest in play-acting.

FRANK. Why?

> *Beat.*

I don't get it, you were a / film star -

MARIA. You know you are like a child, picking at a scab. Do you expect some personal message, Mr Luckett, written in ash? Or are you just a voyeur?

FRANK. A what?

MARIA. A peeping / tom –

FRANK. Hold / on –

MARIA. Or perhaps you are seeking the punchline to a new kraut / joke –

FRANK. Now / wait a bloody –

MARIA. Aren't you afraid the town will whisper about you and the old crone / on the cliff – ?

FRANK. I don't give a fuck what they –

MARIA. No, no of course, they have sent you. The Rotary Club. You are jealous because the tragedy is ours. It is somehow a German tragedy and you all resent that, because in your miserable lives nothing happens, nothing happens that is not small –

MARIA *throws drink into* FRANK*'s face.*

FRANK. Thank you.

MARIA. You're welcome.

MARIA *suddenly lurches for him, hits him across shoulder with walking stick.*

FRANK. Aagh – !

Catches him on ear.

Aagh, you fucking madwoman – !

Swinging wildly at him.

Jesus wept – !

MARIA *staggers after him. Starts to fall, drops her stick.* FRANK *has to leap forward to catch her. Struggles to keep her upright.*

FRANK. Oh fucking hell, fucking hell – !

He slips, begins to fall. She slides from his grasp. They both end up on ground.

My fucking ear –

MARIA *laughs.*

MARIA. I'm sorry. It was meant to be your / nose.

FRANK. Bloody / madwoman –

MARIA. I was trying so hard to hate / you –

FRANK. You're drunk –

MARIA. We've not started, surely? I have Schnapps / in the house –

FRANK. You're joking –

MARIA. Come, I insist we are completely rat-arsed. Stop sulking –

MARIA *offers bottle.* FRANK *doesn't take it. Pause.*

Oh very well, Mr Luckett. Let us rake over the coals with our bare feet. Who cares anyway? It's only good for gossip now. The war of secrets on the cliff. On one side, the ancient kraut film star with a shameful history. On the other, the good doctor who could bear it no longer –

She laughs. Drinks from bottle. Beat.

MARIA. Annie found some of the letters I wrote to my mother from Berlin. She confronted me with them. So I am obliged to describe to her a single day I spend in the company of Adolf Hitler. There. The banality of confession.

Beat.

FRANK. Bollocks. This is bollocks –

MARIA. What is bollocks, Mr Luckett – ?

FRANK. Adolf fucking Hitler. / Jesus –

MARIA. He was a man. He offered me a job. He introduced me to my husband. And I never saw him again.

MARIA *finishes the bottle.*

Look at us. We are lying at the bottom of the bottle, Mr Luckett. The dregs.

KATHLEEN *approaches.*

Kathleen? We were only talking. We were having an adult discussion. We are adults –

Beat.

Kathleen, it is not polite, this eavesdroppping. What would your mother say – ?

KATHLEEN. Is my mum dead because of you?

MARIA. No.

Pause.

KATHLEEN. I'm going into Padstow.

KATHLEEN *goes off.*

MARIA. You and your filthy / cherry blossom –

FRANK. Don't you blame me, Mrs / Schweniger –

MARIA. Help me up –

FRANK. I gotta / go –

MARIA. Help me up – !

FRANK. Is that an order?

FRANK *collecting* BILLY. BILLY *keeps wooden box.*

MARIA. I will not be ashamed.

FRANK. You people –

MARIA. I will not reinvent my past simply to accommodate your bigotry, Mr Luckett. I won't allow you to leave behind the whiff of some half-baked English Rotary Club / morality –

FRANK. We're not English, we're / Cornish –

MARIA. I was an actress. That is all. I belonged, like millions, to the party of complete indifference. But it is the war. You are alone in Berlin. You are young. Hungry. And you will work. One day, without warning, a black car comes to your door. The black car takes you to the circus. For a short time, you become a clown in the circus.

FRANK. Fucking hell – this idn' juss about you, you selfish cow. What about her? What about Kathleen – ?

MARIA. Get out! Get out. And take your idiot son with you.

Silence. FRANK and BILLY go off.

MARIA. Oh Mr Luckett, I –

MARIA's eyes rest on patch of scorched grass.

Damn you . . . !

Shaft of light revealing Hauptsturmfuhrer in 'SS' uniform. He lifts MARIA, leads her gently to wheelchair.

SOLDIER. Du siehst alt aus, Maria –

Settles her into wheelchair.

Du solltest wirklich mehr auf dich aufpassen.

Pushes her to cliff-edge. They stare out to sea.

PART TWO

EIGHT

the arithmetic of memory

MARIA *dreams. Berlin Chancellery.* MARIA *in wheelchair on verandah. Inside,* HITLER *playing piano. Schumann's 'Der Dichter Spricht' from his 'Kinderszenen'.* SECRETARY *there. A long table. A* SERVANT *decorating it with food.* HITLER *makes a mistake.*

HITLER. Verdammt –

Tries again. Another mistake.

Verdammt –

Tries again. The piece falls apart completely.

Verfluchte Scheisse.

Leaps up.

Wo sind meine Ärzte? Wo sind meine verfluchten Ärzte – !

SECRETARY *runs off.*

Wenn ich einen Arzt rufe, dann erwarte ich den Arzt hier – und zwar sofort – !

HITLER *goes to table. About to pour himself a fruit juice. Picks up plate instead.*

Was ist das? Was soll das sein? Komm her. Wie würdest du das bezeichnen? Die Meinung eines Experten wenn ich bitten darf.

SERVANT. Huhn.

HITLER. Wie bitte?

SERVANT. Huhn – ?

HITLER *tosses plate onto ground.*

HITLER. Falls ich dich noch einmal dabei erwische, dass du mir Fleisch auf den Tisch stellst, dann werde ich meine Hunde zu dir nach Hause schicken um deine Mutter zu vögeln. Ist das verstanden?

SERVANT. Jawohl, mein Führer.

SECRETARY (*entering*). Doctor Morell is on / his way.

HITLER. This is excellent. What's in it?

SERVANT. Orange and apricot, sir.

HITLER. I love fruit juice. We will have an 'SS' campaign to popularize fruit juice. Write that down.

SECRETARY *makes a note.*

Get out.

SERVANT *hurries off, taking plates of chicken with him.* HITLER *throws off jacket, rolls up shirt sleeve.* MORELL *enters, carrying black bag.*

MORELL. Sorry, sorry – oh dear. Oh dear, I'm late. Late, late, late. Oh dear. / Where am I – ?

HITLER. Are you hiding from me?

MORELL. I've been – uh – in the toilet, sir –

HITLER. You're repulsive –

MORELL. I'm not very well –

HITLER. Ribbentrop has complained in triplicate about your offensive odour.

MORELL. It's my tummy –

HITLER. My pulse is seventy-four.

MORELL. Seventy-four?

MORELL *taking* HITLER*'s pulse.*

HITLER. It was seventy-two at four a.m. My temperature is ninety-nine. It's been up and down all night.

MORELL. I have something / new today –

HITLER. My little fat slug – take a bath. Just once a week will do. And eat wholemeal bread. Get some of this off –

Pinches him.

It's disgusting. Wars are for thin people –

MORELL. Seventy-five –

HITLER. Someone is going to think you don't believe in the war.

MORELL. Uh – how about a nice injection?

MORELL *fumbles with syringe.*

HITLER. I'm not ill, am I?

MORELL. Out of the question –

HITLER. I am not in any sense of the term, ill?

MORELL. You are not ill by any contemporary definition –

HITLER. Hm. Run the contemporary definition by me once more.

MORELL. It is my feeling / that –

HITLER. Feeling, feeling, feeling – ?

MORELL. Scientific feeling – that illness is a disorder of the uh – of the uh, of the uh – can't find a vein – of the uh – personality –

HITLER. Personality disorder.

MORELL. Yes – every social deviation, in fact –

HITLER. Is an illness –

MORELL. That is the current scientific opinion –

HITLER. Which makes it an impossibility that I –

MORELL. In your case, sir, a scientific impossibility –

HITLER. Thank God for medical science.

MORELL *searching* HITLER*'s arm.*

HITLER. There. There's one. What about that one?

MORELL. Oh yes, that's a nice one –

HITLER. Get it in. Brack's coming. We have to go over the film with what's-her-face and I will be a picture of health. He was never ill!

MORELL *struggles to get needle in.*

MORELL. It's so exciting. The movies – !

HITLER. Come on –

MORELL. Oh dear, go in, go in, get in, you – oh . . .

HITLER. What?

MORELL. I've bent the needle.

HITLER. You arse. Give it here –

HITLER *snatches syringe, shoves needle into his arm.*
MORELL *goes to black bag. Takes out bottles of pills.*

MORELL. Vitamultinforte, as usual. Intelan. Eupaverin. Extra vitamin C. Calcium. Pervitin. Some of my own penicillin, which is lovely. I'm keeping you on the Ultraseptyl because it worked so well on Doctor Goebbels. His skin's completely cleared –

HITLER. What's in this?

MORELL *gives* HITLER *plate of pills.* HITLER *crams in a mouthful.* MORELL *takes syringe.*

MORELL. Ah – this is new. Orchikrin. It's the hormone of youth. I've extracted it myself from the heart, liver and testicles of an ox –

HITLER. You squirt liquid animal into me?

Beat.

I'm a vegetarian!

Beat.

What's the point?

MORELL. Forgive / me, I –

HITLER. What is the point?

MORELL. I'm sorry, I'm sorry –

HITLER. Don't apologize, you fat slug! Wallowing in guilt. It is weakness. It is inauthentic conduct. Christ Almighty, am I the only one around here who bothers to read Heidegger?

MORELL. I'm sorry –

HITLER *slaps him.*

Sorry –

HITLER *slaps him again.*

HITLER. Stop being flaccid! You have to earn redemption through strength! Look at you –

HITLER *kisses* MORELL *on head.*

HITLER. Forget it. Go and fetch my leeches, there's a good chap. My head's exploding.

MORELL *hurries to bag. Removes some pots.*

Did you know, Himmler's been recommending we set up homoeopathic field hospitals on every front? Hardly the place for a two hour consultation, I'd have thought.

BRACK *enters in medical officer uniform, clutching pile of papers.*

Where have you been?

BRACK. How are we today?

HITLER. What do you mean?

BRACK. How are we feeling?

HITLER. What are you implying?

Beat.

BRACK. Nothing.

HITLER. Good. Report.

BRACK. I've just completed the appointment of Doctor Mennecke to the Aktion T-4 programme. He is the country's foremost intelligence in the diagnosis of anti-social behaviour and political unreliability. He can spot a Jew at ten paces.

HITLER. Is that a joke?

BRACK. Yes.

HITLER. Did you find it funny?

MORELL. No.

HITLER. No. I thought it in bad taste. It suggests you don't take the health of the nation seriously.

BRACK. It's well-known I have no sense of humour.

BRACK gives HITLER papers.

HITLER. Tuck in.

BRACK and MORELL fill plates with food. HITLER studies papers.

HITLER. Did you hear my recital?

BRACK. Your playing is sublime –

MORELL. Your interpretation of Schumann is indescribably moving –

HITLER. I surround myself with crawlers. Such is the art of political longevity. Write that down.

SECRETARY makes a note. HITLER notices something on BRACK's plate.

HITLER. Don't eat those. They're my leeches.

BRACK. The new medicine is so advanced –

HITLER. Indeed it is. We used to import our leeches from Brazil, didn't we Morell? Now we breed our own. Those are German leeches.

MORELL eating heartily.

MORELL. I say – can anyone name an English composer?

HITLER laughs with MORELL.

HITLER. I've been working on some stuff by Mahler.

Beat. BRACK *and* MORELL *looking worried.*

BRACK. Mahler? Isn't / he a – ?

HITLER. His songs fascinate me. 'Under the linden tree, which snowed its blossoms down on me, I knew nothing of life's pain . . . .' Like scabs, you can't help picking at them. You lift a scab and there inside, like a maggot in a rotting corpse, quite dazzled by the light, a little Jew, composing. Of course it's our duty to transcend the unfortunate darkness of Mahler the man, to a German spirituality of sound that he, in his Jewishness, could never have envisaged. Failing that we'll just pretend someone else wrote them.

MORELL. Brilliant.

Pause. HITLER *studying papers.* BRACK *watching nervously.*

BRACK. The preliminary target for the programme is seventy-two thousand radical disinfections. Which is calculated on the basis of the ratio 1000:10:5:1. This means that in every thousand German citizens, there presently exist ten who are physically or mentally unproductive. Out of those ten, five will require residential psychiatric care. We have excellent facilities at Grafeneck and Hadamar. Once installed, the five residents undergo a strenuous and rational programme of care, devised by Doctor Mennecke. It will be discovered that of the five, one is irretrievably dysfunctional. That one – will be granted the right to die.

MORELL. You know, I love numbers. That was like a beautiful painting somehow consisting entirely of arithmetic.

HITLER. How many disinfections has the programme managed so far?

BRACK. Well, at Hadamar / we –

HITLER. What is the total number?

BRACK. Five thousand, two hundred children.

Beat.

HITLER. That's it, is it? Five thousand, two hundred eliminations?

Beat.

HITLER. How many sterilizations?

BRACK. We're still, uh, / collating –

HITLER. The Americans have done over thirty thousand –

BRACK. I have established, however, a new Committee for the Scientific Registration of Serious Hereditarily and Congenitally based / Illnesses –

HITLER. The Americans legalized it in nineteen hundred and seven –

BRACK. Uh – on page ten you'll find I've calculated to two decimal places the precise quantities of bread, marmalade, sausage and margarine that will be saved by the programme –

HITLER. We are over thirty years behind America –

BRACK. Yes, but I estimate that by nineteen forty-one, with the help of the film, of course, we will have successfully disinfected –

HITLER. We are being humiliated by a country full of charlatans, pimps and niggers!

HITLER *throws papers in* BRACK*'s face. She scrambles after them.*

MORELL. Doctor Goebbels / says –

BRACK. I am convinced our methods of selection and isolation will limit collateral damage to the Aryan populace / to an absolute minimum.

MORREL. Doctor Goebbels says the film is a fundamental / contribution –

HITLER. Goebbels says. I know what Goebbels says. 'The best propaganda works imperceptibly' – which coming from a man with a club-foot is rather whimsical. It is imperative this film is a success.

HITLER *looks at* MARIA *out on verandah.*

HITLER. So, Brack. Is she suitable?

BRACK. She comes highly recommended.

HITLER. How old?

BRACK. Nineteen –

HITLER. Good tits.

BRACK. Indeed –

HITLER. But does she understand the essential purpose of the film?

BRACK. She said she found it very moving.

HITLER. Did she? Bring her in.

MORELL *fetches* MARIA. HITLER *picks up pot of leeches.*

MORELL. May I present – Maria Hausmann.

HITLER. Hallo. How are you? So sorry to keep you waiting. Maria, that's charming. Isn't it, Morell? A charming name. Getting into the part already, I see. I like that. We all greatly admire your work. These are my leeches, look.

Beat.

What do you know of the world, Maria? Is that a cruel question? You are still so young.

Beat.

Would you like some strawberries? I'm sorry, there's no cream. I don't believe in it. Dietary ostentation is bad for society. Isn't it, doctor?

MORELL *gives* MARIA *bowl of strawberries.*

MORELL. My problems are wholly glandular, Miss Hausmann, and I am big-boned –

HITLER *takes a strawberry from* MARIA*'s bowl.*

HITLER. Mmmn. I've had them in the cold store.

Beat.

Maria. The film. Do you understand why Hanna wants to kill herself?

MARIA. Yes.

HITLER. Good. Good. Do you have the outline there, Brack?

BRACK *finds papers.*

BRACK. Yes, it's a synthesis of, uh, two popular genres. The love story –

MORELL. 'Ménage a trois – '

BRACK. Quite. And of course the court-room drama –

MORELL. Oh that's always gripping –

BRACK. The central plot revolves around the professor, his beautiful young wife, Hanna –

HITLER. Our beautiful young actress, perhaps –

BRACK. And the family doctor – who realizes that Hanna is developing Multiple Sclerosis –

MORELL. Poor Hanna.

BRACK. We follow the desperate attempts of the professor to find a cure in his laboratory. While the doctor tries everything to alleviate Hanna's suffering and torment –

MORELL. As it slowly dawns on him that he may be falling in love with her –

BRACK. It is hopeless. At Hanna's behest, the professor administers an overdose –

HITLER. Yes, she begs him –

BRACK. The doctor plays the piano in the next room.

MORELL. He weeps.

BRACK. He still refuses to accept the necessity of mercy.

HITLER. I think the doctor has to be playing Schumann.

BRACK. Yes.

SECRETARY *makes a note.*

MORELL. What about the court-room?

BRACK. Ah. Hanna's brother accuses the professor of murdering her for money. The case goes to court. We watch the jurors. They are stricken with indecision. Suddenly we cut to the face of a young man. A Party member. His voice rings with conviction. Of course the professor must be released! He has done nothing wrong! After all, Hanna was irredeemable. Invalid. It is right and just that the professor removed her from society! The young man is a teacher. A true civilization, he pronounces, is one that knows how to deal rationally with its impurities. The other jurors are silent. Such blatant fanaticism, surely it is misplaced? How can we possibly forgive the professor such a crime? Surely life is sacrosanct? And then an old man slowly stands. A retired Prussian major. The major is dignified and calm. Yet his eyes prick with tears. Yes, he says, quietly. Life. But what had Hanna to live for? An existence without life. Years of gradual, humiliating decline. Unable to love. Unable to be loved. A pitiful creature. Ask yourselves. What did she want? The major looks the teacher in the eye. This is not merely a question of ideology. It is a question of compassion. He says –

HITLER. He says – 'I am an old soldier. I know what I am talking about. The state which demands from us the duty to die, must also give us the right to die'.

BRACK. And the professor is acquitted.

MORELL. He loved Hanna and he must go free.

HITLER. The old soldier is a brilliant touch. A master-stroke. Joseph will love that.

Beat.

I'm sorry, would you mind?

HITLER *takes leeches from pot.*

My head is always so bad in the afternoons. My ears buzz incessantly.

He places leech on each cheek.

Aaah. Nature's apostles.

Beat.

It isn't simply a film we are making, Maria. Do you see? We are crawling moment by moment in the tracks of God. The truth.

BRACK. Which naturally consists in what benefits the country.

MORELL. Your health does not belong to you, Maria.

HITLER. You deal in truth, my dear. It is your vocation. This film will be a great work of art. I believe we measure the health of a civilization by the art it produces. Don't you?

Beat.

You can get up now and walk away. Or will you help us?

Beat.

MARIA. Yes, I'm – honoured. Very honoured. Thank you –

HITLER. No, no, no. Not at all, my dear. Thank you.

Beat.

Thank you!

Waves SECRETARY *away. She exits.*

Morell –

Flicks his head to send MORELL *hurrying out.*

I have someone rather special I want you to meet –

He calls off.

Otto! Otto, would you come in please!

SECRETARY *and* OTTO *enter.* OTTO *is the uniformed captain from end of part one.*

HITLER. Come, let me introduce you. This is someone very dear to us. Maria -

BRACK. Hausmann.

HITLER. Maria Hausmann. Actress. Maria, this is Captain Otto Schweniger. Presently in command of the Community Patients

Transport Service at Hadamar. I'm keeping Otto away from the front, because he's a budding baritone, and I'm nurturing him.

MORELL *enters clutching framed painting.* HITLER *presents* MARIA *with it.*

And this is for you, my dear. It's a little something I knocked up, oh, years ago. A small token of our gratitude. I call it 'The Will in Nature'.

HITLER *moving to piano.*

Now then. Otto and I have laid on a little entertainment, in anticipation of a successful afternoon.

MORELL. Splendid!

BRACK. Bravo!

HITLER. Do you sing, Maria?

MARIA *nods.*

We'll make an evening of it, just the three of us. What do you say?

To MORELL *and* BRACK.

HITLER. Leave.

MORELL *and* BRACK *go off.*

HITLER. We've only had time to go through this once, mind –

HITLER *accompanies* OTTO *as he sings 'Die Zwei Blauen Augen', from Mahler's 'Lieder eins Fahrenden Gesellen'.*

When they finish, HITLER *goes off, leaving* OTTO *and* MARIA *alone.* OTTO *stands behind her, as for end of Part One.*

NINE

indigestion

Beach at foot of cliff-top garden. MARIA *in wheelchair, holding* HITLER *painting.* JUDITH *there. Barefoot. Open beach robe. Sunglasses and bikini. Small picnic hamper and rug. Some distance away,* FRANK *sitting on a rock, tossing pebbles absently into sea.* KATHLEEN *enters, disorientated for a moment, seeing* JUDITH.

KATHLEEN (*quietly*). Mum – ?

JUDITH *turns to her.*

JUDITH. Hi. Glad you could make it.

KATHLEEN *walks away.*

She hasn't said a goddam word to me since I got / here –

MARIA. Let her get used to the idea. After all, / she's never laid eyes –

JUDITH. You try explaining who I am – ?

MARIA. She knows who you are –

JUDITH. I doubt that. Look at her, she doesn't know shit.

Beat.

Hey kid, you wanna come start the picnic? You wanna get the old picnic going? Open a bottle of wine, maybe?

KATHLEEN *ignores her.*

JUDITH. You know, at some point someone's gotta tell her to get over it.

MARIA. She is getting / over it –

JUDITH. Yeah but I think she should be over it. She's not grieving for Annie, she's grieving for herself.

MARIA. Is that so wrong?

JUDITH. I'm not saying it's wrong. I'm saying maybe it's getting a little indulgent.

MARIA. It's normal.

JUDITH. Well as long as she's normal, right? That's the main thing.

JUDITH *shakes out rug, spreads it.*

Here okay? Where's the sewage outlet round here – ?

MARIA *rubbing leg, in pain.*

Hey – ? Hey, you okay?

MARIA *waves her away.*

Is it bad?

MARIA. Yes.

Beat.

JUDITH. I wish you'd let me do something –

MARIA. Like what?

Beat.

JUDITH. At least let me take this thing outta your way –

JUDITH *takes painting.*

MARIA. Don't touch it –

JUDITH. You've been carrying it around for days, mom. What the hell is it, anyway? Cornish art? The Cornish School? Am I right? What they call it, 'Kindergarten Kitsch' – ?

MARIA. Please. Give it back –

JUDITH *returns painting.*

JUDITH. You wanna cigarette?

She lights cigarette.

You taken any advice about your diet? I've seen it make a difference. At the Foundation –

MARIA. Really –

JUDITH. Yeah, really. Michael's set up cancer treatment programmes entirely centred upon diet and meditation –

MARIA. Good for Michael –

JUDITH. It is good, isn't it? It's a question of attitude. As Michael says, there's no point punishing yourself –

MARIA. Oh come, Judith. You think I'm doing this to my body deliberately?

JUDITH. It happens.

MARIA. Stupid.

JUDITH. Okay. Okay, I'm not trying to convert you –

KATHLEEN *approaches* FRANK.

KATHLEEN. Where's Billy?

FRANK. With his mother.

JUDITH. Michael built the Foundation with his own hands –

KATHLEEN. I wanna see him.

FRANK. Why?

JUDITH. 'Course that whole twenties thing in California, 'The Foundation for Human Improvement'? That was truly his inspiration –

KATHLEEN. I wanna see him. He took the box –

FRANK. Did he? What box?

KATHLEEN. 'Tis mine. I want it back –

FRANK. They're coming home tonight.

KATHLEEN *sits near* FRANK.

JUDITH. Michael's into germ-plasm theory right now. Don't ask.
But he's a great healer, mom. I watched him teach a dying man
how to fall in love with his disease. Maybe not something a
worn-out old allopath like Annie would condone, but it works.
People like it.

Beat.

I guess it must be genetic, huh? The way me and Annie both
wind up in the caring business? You give birth to a doctor, and
I end up fucking one.

Starts laying out picnic food on rug.

Now what have we got here. We got ham on rye, that's genuine
Cornish rye from Mr Bun the baker. Then there's cucumber and
tomato on white with my own garlic mayonnaise. Or we got
bagels with salmon and cream cheese. What the hell.

Takes out bottle of wine.

Here we go, a quaint bottle of Eurotiddle from 'the post office'
– in deference to The Fatherland. Or beer. I'll go for a beer.

JUDITH *opens bottle of beer. Drinks. Puts bagel on plate,
offers it to* MARIA.

Bagel?

MARIA. I'm not hungry.

JUDITH. Not hungry? Will you have a beer – ? How about you
kid? You go for a beer and a bagel – ?

Beat.

Who is that guy? Friend of the family – ?

MARIA. Mr Luckett – ? Won't you join us, Mr Luckett – ?

Beat.

Please – come and drink a beer with us.

Pause. FRANK *walks over.*

JUDITH. Hi.

JUDITH *offers* FRANK *plate of sandwiches.*

Cucumber. My own mayonnaise. You'll love it –

FRANK *refuses.*

MARIA. Mr Luckett used to bring me fish.

JUDITH. No! A real Cornish fisherman? Jeez, wait till I tell the folks back home –

FRANK. Oh yeah – my family go all the way back to Galilee.

JUDITH. Is that so?

MARIA. But now perhaps Mr Luckett does not like the sea so much –

FRANK. I love the sea. The sea's my wife –

MARIA. Oh now this I think is the genuine bollocks. You are a bad fisherman –

FRANK. Which tosser said that – ?

MARIA. You. They are going to take your boat away, aren't they – ?

FRANK. They already took it.

MARIA. Oh –

FRANK. The bank took it. I'm finished.

MARIA. Oh no –

FRANK. I'm juss fifty foot of wood, see. I can't compete with a ninety foot Spaniard made of steel. Can I?

Beat.

And 'tis the world, idn' it miss? Compete or die?

JUDITH. Right.

MARIA. I'm sorry, Mr Luckett –

FRANK. Why? What have you done?

MARIA. Can I help? Is there nothing I can do – ?

FRANK. You think Frank Luckett would come crawling to the fucking krauts?

Beat.

MARIA. How will you manage?

FRANK. I expect we'll get by, won't we?

MARIA. But what about George? / Surely he – ?

FRANK. I can't carry him no more. He's out on his own, like the rest of us. Maybe God'll find him a way.

Beat.

MARIA. Won't you at least come and see me, Frank? Push me round the garden? Talk to me? I'll let you lift me into the bath. Imagine the secrets I can divulge in / the bath –

FRANK. You think I'm that desperate? You're looking for a servant, Mrs Schweniger –

MARIA. I simply mean if you can't fish, you might as well push –

FRANK. Christ.

Beat.

MARIA. I have wounded your pride. Forgive me. I took you for a man whose pride was drowned long ago. It seems I made a mistake.

Beat.

I made a mistake, Frank. Will you forgive me? Frank – ? Be my friend – ?

FRANK. Mrs Schweniger – my heart is in my boots. My mouth is full of rain.

MARIA. Wait. Please, Frank. Take this –

She holds out Hitler painting.

Go on. Sell it. Someone will say it is very valuable, I promise. Buy your boat –

FRANK *takes painting.*

FRANK. What silly cunt did this?

MARIA. It is a great work of art.

JUDITH. It sure is, Frank.

Beat.

FRANK. She gives me art. She gives me a useless fucking picture. I've got a house full of fucking pictures –

FRANK *hurls painting into the sea. Starts to go. Hesitates by* KATHLEEN.

We killed him, girl. Bright Millar. All of us, we all did it. We made him ashamed to be alive.

FRANK *goes off. Beat.*

JUDITH. He seems a pleasant enough fellow.

JUDITH *takes beer and sandwich to* KATHLEEN.

JUDITH. Here, kid –

KATHLEEN *ignores her.*

Not hungry either, huh?

JUDITH *scoops up sand into her hands, lets it trickle through her fingers.*

I'm making a beautiful waterfall out of sand. Can you see that, Kathleen? Can you do this with your hands?

KATHLEEN. Yeah.

JUDITH. Good. Because we got sand in Santa Monica. The house is only half a block from the beach.

KATHLEEN. Yeah.

Beat.

JUDITH. Do you sleep with your boyfriend? You know, underneath all that grime I bet there's a real pretty girl, just dying to get out? And your hair. I could do a lot with your hair. Like – wash it?

KATHLEEN. Yeah.

Pause.

JUDITH. Listen honey. I lost my dad when I was thirteen, so I know a little. No-one's saying it's easy. But you can't paint the whole world with blame. She knew what she was doing. She made a choice. You know?

KATHLEEN *goes off.*

JUDITH. Is there something wrong with my sandwiches?

Beat.

I have to tell you, mom – I'm beginning to wonder what the fuck I'm doing here.

MARIA. I have no-one, Judith. There is no-one else to ask –

JUDITH. Does that make me the first person you thought of, or the last?

MARIA. Please – I'm asking you to care / for her –

JUDITH. I know what you're asking, believe me –

MARIA. After all, she is my only grandchild –

JUDITH. Yeah. And the thing is, mom – I wonder if I'm quite ready for the burden of parental responsibility.

Assumes Southern accent.

And frankly I'm a tad dismayed you neglected to tell me how the kid just happens to be a retard.

MARIA. She is your sister's daughter.

JUDITH. And I've gotta pick up the pieces, right?

MARIA. You're like a stranger –

JUDITH. Whose fault is that, mom?

MARIA. You call me this 'mom'. It's not the sound of me being your mother.

JUDITH. When were you last my mother?

Pause. JUDITH *has a drink of beer.*

How much does she know?

MARIA. What do / you mean – ?

JUDITH. Did Annie tell her / about you and dad?

MARIA. I don't know what you're / talking about –

JUDITH. Oh come on, mom. I've known for twenty-two years.

MARIA. What – ?

JUDITH *shows* MARIA *delicate chain around her neck.*

JUDITH The baby Jesus. It's silver and ivory. Dad told me he got it from a little crippled German girl he was transporting to one of the hospitals. You know – those long grey mail vans?

Beat.

It's beautiful, isn't it?

Pause.

MARIA. All these years and never / a word –

JUDITH. You chose Annie.

MARIA. No –

JUDITH. You chose Annie and ran away –

MARIA. It wasn't like that –

JUDITH. Hey, I'm not complaining. It's cool. Dad wanted me, didn't he?

Beat.

MARIA. He took you.

JUDITH. Took me – ?

MARIA. He would not let me go otherwise –

MARIA *suddenly hit by fierce pain.*

Urh –

JUDITH. What? What – tell me what to do – shall I hold it here? Does it help if I rub it – ?

JUDITH *gently holds and massages* MARIA*'s leg.*

I'm sorry – I'm sorry, it's me, I – I didn't mean to – you know I didn't come all / this way to –

MARIA. Does it mean nothing to you? Your own sister – ?

JUDITH. I wanted to see my mother. I wanted to tell her she could be proud of me.

JUDITH buries her head in MARIA's lap. Tearful. MARIA finally lays her face on JUDITH's hair.

MARIA. Kathleen mustn't know.

JUDITH. Okay. It's okay. We won't talk about it. We'll never talk about it, I swear.

Pause.

You gotta start taking something for pain –

MARIA. No.

JUDITH. We could get you a nurse –

MARIA. I would murder her.

JUDITH. What about the National Health? This is England for Chrissake –

MARIA. They will put me in a room where everyone is dying. I will say where I die.

JUDITH. You could come / with me –

MARIA. I will never go back to America.

Beat.

JUDITH. What are we gonna do with you, mom? You gotta decide what it is you want –

MARIA reaches into pocket.

MARIA. I want some more of these –

Takes out packet of tablets. JUDITH takes them.

JUDITH. 'Rennie' – ?

MARIA. Yes, I'm running / out –

JUDITH. These are indigestion tablets, / mom,

MARIA. I like them –

JUDITH. that's why they write this word here. See? 'Indigestion' – ?

MARIA. I'm sure they're good for you –

JUDITH chuckles.

JUDITH. Yeah. Yeah okay – I'll buy you some more 'Rennie' –

KATHLEEN *enters.*

Hey Kathleen – will you come and eat something? You gotta eat – she's gotta eat, don't she mom? I know, I know, you're thinking – how can she eat all that shit and stay in shape, right? I'll tell you, Kathleen – it's an act of faith. I don't believe in putting on weight. I look in the mirror, I take off all my clothes, and I do this 'Body Visualization' programme? I say to her, the woman in the mirror, I say – 'If you really love me, you won't get fat'. It's that simple. We call it investing your ego in your body. We can teach you that. But you gotta want it, Kathleen. You gotta want beauty. You gotta want health.

Beat.

Here. I want you to have this –

JUDITH *takes off chain. Puts it round* KATHLEEN*'s neck.*

It's really old. Practically a family heirloom. There. Looks real nice on you.

Beat. KATHLEEN *touching chain.*

Here's the thing. We were just talking about family, weren't we mom? The way it's like a permanent structure. You know – always there for you, even through the bad times.

KATHLEEN *starts to shake.*

And that's what we're offering you back home. A structure. And you know on your birthday? We're all gonna fly down to Disneyland –

KATHLEEN*'s shaking is worse.*

Kathleen – ? What is it – ?

MARIA. Hold her –

JUDITH. Hey – hey, take it easy –

JUDITH *takes* KATHLEEN *by shoulders.*

JUDITH. Take it easy, kid – stand still – stand still, Kathleen!

JUDITH *slaps her.*

Get a holda yourself. Listen to me. There's nothing wrong with you. Kathleen, get over it.

KATHLEEN *pushes away. Runs off. Beat.*

Now what did I do? What the fuck did I do?

TEN

lac caninum

BILLY *sitting on his bed. Small wooden box in his lap. He rolls glass bottle gently in his hands.* KATHLEEN *there.*

KATHLEEN. 'Tis an old feeding bottle, Billy.

> BILLY *nods.*

I found out all about it. She knew I would. I think this one was made about 1790. There was this superstition years ago, if you're breast-feeding you mustn't fuck or else your milk'll go bad. And another one said if you get pregnant when you're still breast-feeding, the new baby gets born strange in the head.

BILLY *nods.* KATHLEEN *takes brass ring from box.*

The rich men bought this special gift-set for their wives. Feeding bottle – and weaning ring. Careful. It has spikes in it, this one. See? The mother puts it over her nipple. The baby sucks and gets the milk, but only if it can bear the pain of the spikes in its lips. You can increase the length of the spikes, so the harder the baby sucks, the deeper they dig in. Eventually, the pain of the spikes is greater than the pleasure of the milk. Pain teaches the baby to say no.

Pause. KATHLEEN *replaces ring and bottle in box.*

She left me behind, Billy. How could she do that?

ELEVEN

a shaming

KATHLEEN *dreams. St. Nun's Pool Asylum. She sings Bright's song.*

KATHLEEN. 'Oh come all you young men
With your wicked ways
And sow all your wild oats
In your youthful days
That we may live happy
That we may live happy
That we may live happy
When we grow old . . . '

> BRIGHT *is there, beaten and trembling. Drifting in and out of delirium.*

Oh God – what have they done to you – ?

KATHLEEN *runs and holds him.*

We'll run – we'll run – we can run for ever, Bright – till we catch fire –

BRIGHT. Too late –

Huge terrible sound. The place seemingly cracks apart. Intimidating shape appearing from below. The KEEPER *is there, assembling medical apparatus. A seat with leather straps.*

KATHLEEN. I'm not leaving / you –

BRIGHT. I'm theirs, girl! They own me – !

Noise off. CHYLE *laughing.*

BRIGHT. Don't let 'em see you. Hide. Hide – !

KATHLEEN *hides in shadows.*

CHYLE (*off*). Of course, my erstwhile colleagues regard me as some kind of witch. They would have me sent back to a life of midwifery –

DILL (*off*). Shame on / them –

CHYLE *and* DILL *entering.*

CHYLE. All I want, all I've ever wanted – is to be called 'doctor' by my peers.

Pause. DILL *surveying surroundings apprehensively.*

My little garden. My little garden of judgement.

DILL. Yes –

CHYLE. Welcome.

DILL. Thank you, my dear.

CHYLE *assembling contraption. Preparing medical machinery and equipment.* KEEPER *assisting in construction. Something nightmarish forming.*

CHYLE. My own design –

DILL. It is – modern –

CHYLE. Revolutionary –

DILL. Revolutionary, yes. May I – ?

CHYLE. Please don't touch.

DILL. Sorry –

CHYLE. It's a delicate instrument –

DILL. Yes. Quite –

CHYLE. The subject sits here, secured by these straps –

Nods to KEEPER. KEEPER *ties* BRIGHT *into seat of machine.*

Bright Millar. One of my boys –

DILL. Charming name.

CHYLE. Bright? May I present the Lord Bishop of Truro, Stanley Dill – ?

DILL (*to* BRIGHT). Do call me Stan –

CHYLE. He's come to observe the fruits of our labours together.

DILL. Looking forward to it –

CHYLE. You might be better standing over there –

DILL. Absolutely. Wherever, my dear –

CHYLE *talking as she busies herself with machine and equipment.*

CHYLE. It came to me in The Congo –

DILL. India – ?

CHYLE. Africa.

DILL. Same difference –

CHYLE. Watching a child with some evil deformity being driven into a river by all the old women. And afterwards burned on a hill –

DILL. Oh dear –

CHYLE. And yet within the barbarity of that, do you see – ? Something humane. Something civilized –

DILL. Absolution – ?

CHYLE. I prefer redemption.

DILL. Ah –

CHYLE. Salvation through punishment –

DILL. Yes that's much better –

CHYLE. It was then I knew, Stanley. From that moment, my life's work would always turn upon a single question: to what purpose the curing of a ravaged body, if the soul remains in torment?

DILL. Indeed –

CHYLE. It is empty. We are empty, you and I. Unless we learn to treat the soul –

DILL. The soul, yes.

Beat.

How – uh – how does it work?

CHYLE. First the paintings.

KEEPER *shows series of paintings to* BRIGHT. *Images projected on walls all around the machine.*

DILL. Landscapes – ?

CHYLE. The therapeutic power of art. They beautify the boy's experience. Caress his soul. At the same time we are filled with revulsion. The thought of losing our English paradise. A terrible warning, Stanley. The price of unGodly pleasures –

DILL. Yes of course, in the midst of beauty we are in anguish, I like / that –

BRIGHT. I want Harry –

DILL. He wants / Harry –

CHYLE. He means Horatio. The boy claims he was on board 'The Victory', / swears

BRIGHT. I was –

CHYLE. he tended the great man's body –

BRIGHT. I held him –

DILL. Not Horatio / Nelson – ?

BRIGHT. I washed his lilywhite / flesh –

CHYLE. It seems they preserved him in a gherkin / barrel –

BRIGHT. He had such small hands. I kissed his sores –

DILL. Kissed his – ? What does he mean? Is he saying Horatio / Nelson – ?

BRIGHT. He sucked my cock –

DILL. Good God –

CHYLE. He craves our hatred.

DILL. Why?

CHYLE. So he can forgive himself.

DILL. Fascinating –

CHYLE. It's symptomatic. Classical tertiary stage.

DILL. The church is broad-minded. We are men after all –

CHYLE. He's the perfect subject, Stanley. Watch. Concentrate, Bright. I want you to remember our lessons together. Now. What is syphilis?

Beat.

What is syphilis? / Say it –

KEEPER *jabs* BRIGHT *with stick.*

KATHLEEN (*quietly*). Don't –

BRIGHT. 'Syphilis – is the scourge of history – '

CHYLE. Good boy. And? There's a plan, / isn't there – ?

KATHLEEN (*quietly*). Mum, don't –

BRIGHT. 'The – Divine Plan – '

CHYLE. Because – ?

KATHLEEN (*quietly*). Let him go, mum, please –

CHYLE. Because syphilis is the finger of God. Say it. Say it – !

KATHLEEN *runs out of shadows.*

KATHLEEN. Don't help her, Bright – !

KEEPER *intercepts* KATHLEEN, *hand on her throat, forcing her to the ground. Stands over her.*

BRIGHT. 'Syphilis is the finger of God.'

CHYLE. Well done. You see? They can be taught. Even the fallen mind can be disciplined.

CHYLE *ascends back of machine. Music insinuating.*

Imagine. Truro Cathedral. The subject addresses the congregation from the machine. Your congregation, Stanley. Perhaps a placard round his neck –

DILL. Good idea –

CHYLE. An island of shame. At the centre of paradise, the fallen creature, shamed –

DILL. Yes –

CHYLE. Ashamed. Suffering for us. The congregation all around –

DILL. Television –

CHYLE. Learning. Changing. You're in the pulpit –

DILL. Yes –

CHYLE. Speak to your people – !

DILL. Yes – !

>DILL *inspired by* CHYLE*'s enthusiasm, as if addressing his congregation. Music building.*

CHYLE. Tell them about the violation of man's sexual nature – !

DILL. Yes, the offence against nature's laws – !

CHYLE. The eternal blackness of his nights – !

DILL. We call the wrath of God upon our heads – !

CHYLE. People are weeping – !

DILL. They cry out, 'Why is God punishing us – ?'

CHYLE. And you say – ?

DILL. You are not devoted to cleanliness! Therefore you cannot be devoted to God – !

CHYLE. Good! Now they beg forgiveness – !

>CHYLE *preparing drill mechanism.*

DILL. I cannot forgive! God has put your flesh into the hands of Satan – !

CHYLE. Excellent – !

DILL. You have drowned your souls in a sea of pleasure! And then I take pity – I weep for them –

CHYLE. I am ready –

DILL. I console. I comfort. I give succour. And I say, this – this is the shaming of Bright Millar – !

KATHLEEN. No –

DILL. Bear witness! For his shame can be your moral strength – !

CHYLE. I open a sluice for the Devil, and take the evil into my mouth. I drill into the skull -

DILL. My God –

KATHLEEN. No – !

>*Music reaches climax.* CHYLE *drills into* BRIGHT*'s skull.* BRIGHT *screams. Drilling completed,* CHYLE *puts device to* BRIGHT*'s skull, sucks. Blows spout of liquid away, igniting great burst of flame from the ground where* ANNIE *burned herself. Silent aftermath.* CHYLE *descending.*

DILL. He isn't . . . he isn't dead – ?

CHYLE. He is cleansed.

>*Beat.*

DILL. He does die, though – ?

CHYLE. Eventually, yes.

DILL. Good. Good. Because it might seem somewhat of a theological contradiction, if what we know to be Divine retribution was suddenly thwarted by a miraculous return to health.

CHYLE. The cure enables him to come to his inevitable end in peace.

DILL. Quite. Quite –

CHYLE. He will become a martyr to all the good children who have drunk from the poisoned fountain of life.

KATHLEEN (*quietly*). Let him down, mum –

CHYLE *nods to* KEEPER. KEEPER *releases* BRIGHT. *Lays him down.* KATHLEEN *goes to him, holds him.*

CHYLE. Now his soul is free. He is floating, far above us. He has a third eye, fixed on heaven.

DILL. I'm – I'm almost envious.

CHYLE. To know syphilis is to know medicine, Stanley. There is no escape. Everybody dies. That is the truly religious thing about this disease.

DILL. If only my sermons could be hewn from the stone of these walls –

CHYLE. Medicine will become religion. This is the future. Will you help me?

DILL. I assure you, the world will hear of your work – Doctor Chyle.

CHYLE. Thank you.

Beat.

He will sleep now.

CHYLE *and* DILL *starting to go off together.*

DILL. You will have to prepare another, I suppose?

CHYLE. I have several.

DILL. A boy –

CHYLE. Or a girl –

DILL. Oh I think a boy. If I may be permitted an aesthetic preference . . .

They go off.

KATHLEEN. I'm touching your hand. See? I don't mind touching.
No harm. No evil. I'm kissing your hands –

BRIGHT. Harry – ? That you Harry – ? Eh Harry, listen – if
syphilis is the finger of God – whass the rest of Him look like?

The KEEPER *lifts* BRIGHT. *Carries him off.* KATHLEEN
helpless. Soundtrack of HITLER *in mid-rant, loud and slow.*
HITLER *sounding like some strange animal, growling and
moaning eerily. Mixed in with this, a piano playing Schumann's
'Der Dichter Spricht'.*

TWELVE

more light

*A fisherman , GEORGE LUCKETT, alone. Sings last verse and
refrain of Methodist hymn, 'Let the Lower Lights'.*

GEORGE. Trim your feeble lamp, my brother,
    Some poor sailor, tempest-tossed,
    Trying now to make the harbour,
    In the darkness may be lost.

    Let the lower lights be burning,
    Send a gleam across the wave;
    Some poor fainting, struggling seaman
    You may rescue, you may save.

GEORGE goes.

Simultaneous scene:

Beach at foot of cliff-top garden. Night. Full moon. MARIA
there in wheelchair, smoking one of her cigars. JUDITH *beside
her.*

Fisherman's cottage in Padstow. BILLY*'s bedroom.* BILLY
and FRANK *together, sitting on bed in silence.* BILLY *staring
out of window.*

FRANK. Your mother's asleep. Told her about the boat. She's
living in another world.

Beat.

Anyway she's sleeping now.

They sit. Beat. JUDITH *lights cigarette.*

MARIA. Goethe. Remember? 'Wer nicht von dreitausend / Jahren – '

JUDITH. Hey. You'll have to speak my language.

Beat.

MARIA. Tch. 'People who cannot give an account to themselves of the past three thousand years remain in darkness, without experience, living from day to day.'

Beat.

JUDITH. No. I don't remember, mom.

MARIA *smiles.*

MARIA. Is anything worth remembering?

JUDITH. Sure.

MARIA. History. Endlessly recycling the same jokes, the same petty miseries, staggering from one incurable crisis to the next – it is a farce. Nothing is done. What have we learned really? Nothing.

Beat.

JUDITH. Were you never happy?

MARIA. Of course –

JUDITH. I mean you and dad.

MARIA. Your father's enthusiasms. So tawdry. So predictable. He couldn't wait to get his mitts on Hollywood. He loved it there. It was infectious. It became unbearable.

They smoke. BILLY *goes to window, stares at the sky.*

FRANK. Yeah I know, boy. Sometimes you juss want to stare at the stars. I do that . . .

FRANK *goes to window. Stands beside* BILLY, *stares at the sky.*

I'm on the boat. Coming home. I look up, and – all the birds are going into the stars, and I want to go into the stars . . .

They stare at the sky in silence.

MARIA. You know, in nineteen fifty-six I went to a boxing match, in Berlin –

JUDITH. But you were living here then –

MARIA. I had gone there to meet Brecht. Mother Courage in Düsseldorf. I wanted to discuss the role with him. Of course, he pretended he knew nothing of my past. We talked into the night. He was very troubled. Near death. He was really quite a boring man. So obviously famous, the way he kept repeating himself. He went on and on – 'The new ice age of fascism,

Maria, why can't anyone see it?' The next evening he took me to a beer hall to watch the boxing. The screaming. Our feet thundering on the wooden floor. Brecht studied the boxer's face. The speed of his feet and hands. At one point he turned to me. We were laughing. He shouted – 'Do you have the bug, Maria!' I spent the entire evening watching the audience. The new ice age freezing the air in my lungs. Like eating fruit straight from the fridge.

Beat.

I think that was the happiest night of my life.

Beat. BILLY *goes back to his bed.*

FRANK. I thought I knew what to do, Billy.

MARIA. My Mother Courage was terrible. Hideous.

They smoke in silence. FRANK *stays at window.*

FRANK. We took you fishing. Remember? You were counting the bloody waves. And I thought, how do you count the sea? You took hold of my hand, pulled me to the stern. The waves were chasing after us, and you made me do the counting out loud, till I was shouting. And the waves kept coming. And I was shouting, 'Who the fuck is anyone without the sea!' And you were laughing. And I shouted the numbers for you till I was hoarse.

Beat.

You see, boy – that was my best. I don't know what else there is.

FRANK *stares out of window.* MARIA *stubs out cigar, chuckling.*

MARIA. Goethe's last words. Do you know what they were?

JUDITH. Do you know what a 'boogie-board' is?

Beat.

MARIA. 'Mehr Licht!' More light.

JUDITH. That's nice.

MARIA. Yes, but actually what he said was, 'Macht doch den zweiten Fensterladen auch auf, damit mehr Licht hereinkommt.'

JUDITH. Yeah? What does that mean?

MARIA. Well it sort of means, 'Open the curtains, I can't see a bloody thing in here.'

MARIA *chuckles. Beat.*

Enough.

MARIA *starts to climb out of wheelchair.* JUDITH *stubs out cigarette. Helps* MARIA. MARIA *grips her wrist.*

You promise me she will be safe?

JUDITH. I promise. We'll take good care of her. Okay?

They move slowly.

We'll just keep walking all the way out there, okay? Until we stop, mom. Until we stop . . .

JUDITH *supports* MARIA. *They go off,* MARIA *chuckling to herself.*

MARIA. 'Mehr Licht' . . . 'Mehr Licht' . . .

They are walking into the sea. BILLY *struggles for his words, forces them out.*

BILLY. Wh – wh – wha – what – was her name?

FRANK *stares at him, shocked at his clarity.*

FRANK. What – ?

BILLY. Sh – she – must have – a name.

Beat.

FRANK. The Treyarnon girl – ?

BILLY. You – nnn – never – gg – gg – gave her – a name.

FRANK. Who?

BILLY. Gg – gg – gi – give her back.

Beat.

Gg – give her back – t – to me dad.

FRANK. Kathleen.

BILLY *shakes his head.*

FRANK. What? What – ?

BILLY *looks into* FRANK's *eyes for first time.*

BILLY. My sister.

Pause. FRANK *lifts* BILLY. *Hugs him. Buries* BILLY *in long embrace, holding* BILLY's *face against his chest. Sound of the sea swelling unnaturally.*

THIRTEEN

the question

Cliff-top garden. Night. Full moon. KATHLEEN *sitting near patch of scorched grass, wooden box in her lap.* JUDITH *enters, dripping wet.*

JUDITH. Hey, I just been in the water. It was so warm, Kathleen, it was just like taking a bath.

Beat.

Does it ever cross your mind, other people might suffer because you won't take care of yourself?

Pause. Squats beside KATHLEEN.

Can you hear the planet screaming, Kathleen? Sometimes I wake up at night, in a cold sweat, and I swear I can hear the planet screaming at us.

Beat.

In every five people there are four too many. That's four fifths of the fucking world, Kathleen. What do you make of that? I figure the question here – the question no-one's asking – is who don't we need? Who really don't we need?

Beat.

Someone's gotta start liberating the earth, Kathleen. Or else – where's the future?

She stands.

I'm gonna go pack some suitcases. You'll wanna do your own, right?

JUDITH *starts to go off as* FRANK *enters, carrying* BILLY'*s lifeless body.*

Hi Frank. What the fuck do you want?

JUDITH *passes him, goes off. Pause.*

FRANK. So – so I said to him, we'll go and see the Treyarnon girl now.

FRANK *lays* BILLY *on ground near* KATHLEEN.

I said – I know a place, Billy. There's this woman I knew in school, see. She's got this caff. Up in St Nectan's Glen. 'Tis above the waterfall. 'Tis desolate. I said – we could go there. The three of us. Maybe they'd never find us. You two could teach me. You know, what a good father is. 'Cus I wanna learn, see.

Beat.

What shall we do?

Beat.

I'll leave him here, shall I? Get a doctor. Yeah. Right. Leave him with you.

Beat.

Won't be long. Juss go and get a doctor.

Beat.

I'll tell 'em – something must've happened.

FRANK *goes off. Pause.*

KATHLEEN. Can you smell the sea, Billy?

Beat.

Smells of bad dreams.

FOURTEEN

urlicht

Music. The opening section of Mahler's setting of folk-poem 'Urlicht', from Fourth Movement of his Second Symphony.

KATHLEEN *takes glass bottle from wooden box.*

MARIA *and* OTTO *appear.* MARIA *is nineteen. They are happily walking together. Playful. They stop to kiss.*

KATHLEEN *watches* MARIA *and* OTTO *pass by. They go off.* KATHLEEN *squeezes bottle between her hands. Eventually it breaks. Her hands bleed. She puts her hands to her mouth. She eats the glass.*

The End.